NO MAN IS AN ISLAND

TAVARES GARDINER
NO MAN IS AN ISLAND

TATE PUBLISHING
AND ENTERPRISES, LLC

No Man Is an Island
Copyright © 2013 by Tavares Gardiner. All rights reserved.

No part of this publication may be reproduced, stored in a retrieval system or transmitted in any way by any means, electronic, mechanical, photocopy, recording or otherwise without the prior permission of the author except as provided by USA copyright law.

This book is designed to provide accurate and authoritative information with regard to the subject matter covered. This information is given with the understanding that neither the author nor Tate Publishing, LLC is engaged in rendering legal, professional advice. Since the details of your situation are fact dependent, you should additionally seek the services of a competent professional.

The opinions expressed by the author are not necessarily those of Tate Publishing, LLC.

Published by Tate Publishing & Enterprises, LLC
127 E. Trade Center Terrace | Mustang, Oklahoma 73064 USA
1.888.361.9473 | www.tatepublishing.com

Tate Publishing is committed to excellence in the publishing industry. The company reflects the philosophy established by the founders, based on Psalm 68:11,
"The Lord gave the word and great was the company of those who published it."

Book design copyright © 2013 by Tate Publishing, LLC. All rights reserved.
Cover design by Jeffrey Doblados
Interior design by Caypeeline Casas

Published in the United States of America

ISBN: 978-1-62854-213-4
1. Self-Help / General
2. Self-Help / Personal Growth / Success
13.10.29

DEDICATION

To my beautiful wife, Nicole Gardiner, for being the light that shines in my darkest hours. To my two amazing boys for teaching me to always dream big.

ACKNOWLEDGMENTS

It's a long list of people to thank, but first and foremost, I would like to thank God for the many blessings that he showered on me. Special thanks to the entire Tate Publishing especially to Alana Duffle, Lindsey Marcus & Allen Finch. My wonderful mother, Joya Pennerman, for her love and support, and my father, Vincent Gardiner, for the wisdom he shared daily on those long journeys home. My aunt and uncle, Terry and Derek Benjamin, for the help in molding me to be the young man I am today. My younger brother, Tavano Gardiner, you made me realized that writing is an essential part of my being, love you dearly, bro!

The entire Roker clan, you all played an amazing role in my life, love you all sincerely. Uncle Keith and my remarkable Aunt Sarah, you kept a dude fired up. To the mother of all mothers, Lerlene Pennerman (deceased), for making me understand that company and friends can lead you down the wrong path. Joyce Pennerman (deceased), thank you dearly for always believing in me; I miss you Grammy! Kevin Brown and Winston Pennerman for blessing a young man with a great sense of humor.

The entire Albury family, for showing me a different side of life. To all my siblings, (The Gardiner Crew), you all played a vital role in my life. Mary Flowers (deceased) I miss you Mama! You literally taught me to always walk by faith and not by sight. Pastor Rick Dean and his lovely wife along with the Family of Faith ministry, thank you for your consistent love, support, and most of all your prayers.

Special thanks to everyone that grew up on the street of Bangle dash Crescent, you know who you are! To the whole community of Flamingo Gardens, you help raised a unique individual. Special thanks to my beautiful mother in law, Yvette Minns aka Ms. Minns, for every encouraging word that you have spoken over my life. To all my in-laws in Freeport, Grand Bahama. Uncle Chris you are truly amazing, Elliot and Aahmaud Minns, you both are definitely a special part of my life! Brother Gordon and Sister Pearl, thank you for your endless love.

Special thanks to my spiritual mother, Auntie Pat, you are a true testament of the words standing firm on God's holy Word. Mr. C. Barry, one of the coolest guys I've ever met, thanks a million, bro! My dynamic team and former staff; Odnan Missick, Chernelle Stuart, and Zendall Carey you guys were the best.

Special thanks to Davion Benjiman and Courtnee Romer, let's keep living the life we said we would! Delmaro Stubbs (deceased) and Kano Davis, my two big brothers that help carried me through my transition years. Kendra Thomas and family, for the guidance you gave me through those adverse moments in my life. Clarice Hanna for always seeing beyond my flaws. Branado Brice, I could never stop thanking you, you have been the ultimate angel in my life. Dexter Robinson, words can never express how I feel about our journey, you are truly one of a kind, and I thank you daily.

Saving the best for last, my amazing wife, Nicole Gardiner, I love you dearly. You made every step worth taking, and I appreciate you for that. My two wonderful sons, Tyren and Nyeem Gardiner, the corner stones of my life! To every individual who made this moment possible, I truly thank you for your love and support!

INTRODUCTION

In life, we all dream of traveling different places and becoming people of great prominence, but when given the opportunity, we don't always take advantage of them. There are many reasons why, such as lack of support, fear of failing, low self esteem etc., but most of all, lack of faith—the faith in God, the faith in yourself, and the faith to believe that all things are possible.

I believe that opportunities present themselves many times in life. It's just waiting for us to make that move toward it; whether it's near or far we have to take one step at a time. Setting our goals and aiming directly for it, not wavering or quitting on what you truly believe in. Of course we all have challenges to face, but where there is a will; there is a way. In fact, perseverance plays a vital role in making your dreams a reality. Even Christ Jesus displayed actions of persistence, after being rejected on many occasions; he still press forward toward the mark, and now to this day, he is the great, I am.

My question to you; are you that next great person of prominence; are you being that individual God purpose you to be, well if so let it be known as we all shine our lights, because we are the light of this world.

CHAPTER 1

As I rest my head against my pillow, gazing out my bed room window; I think to myself, Will I ever make it out? Surely the sun is about to set and I don't know if I could stand another taste of what is to come tomorrow. My mother has just finish whooping my back side; the bruises on my skin are severe and it's very difficult for me to lie comfortably. I don't know if to call this abuse or just plain old discipline, maybe it's just me wanting to have my own way, but what is so wrong with wanting to go on the basketball court with my friends?

Before I could utter another word out of my mouth, Mom came storming through the door saying, "Boy get ya ass up and clean these dishes." I responded, "Yes, Mom." Of course with a trembling sound in my voice. As I glance across the dining room table, I can see my younger sister laughing at what had just happen, sometimes I feel like they allow her so much slackness.

About an hour into the evening, I heard T, Demetrio, and Kane bouncing the ball as they arrived from the basketball court, I wish I was there. I could hear the excitement in their voices as they truckle through the yard, so I sneaked to the window and ask T if a lot of guys came out this evening, with such excitement he said, "Yeah, bro! Where were you?" I told him Mom is freaking out again, but anyway, we'll talk later. I wondered to myself if he heard the embarrassment in the tone of my voice, it had to be obvious because I abruptly closed the blinds and slammed myself on to my pillow.

It's 6:30 am, and I can hear the shower running in the bathroom, Shana must be getting ready for school. I know Mom is soon going to bust through my door and tell me to get up, but before she does, I hurry over to the bathroom to drain the lizard.

Seconds after, Shana screams, "You don't know how to knock before entering ay?"

Instantly, I suck my teeth and told her to shut up. "This is really my bathroom." Mom must've heard us bickering because as soon as I stepped outside the bathroom door she was standing right there with a belt in her hand saying, "Hurry up and get your ass in the tub before I cut your skin boy." I think that was the fastest I've ever showered and put on cloths in my life.

After being dropped off to school, I thought about how I can't wait to finish high school. I kept saying to myself it's only one more year before I graduate. Even though being an eleventh-grader has its perks, I'm still exhausted. Okay, not too exhausted to go on our school court during break time. Yes, sir, it's break time, and I'm about to catch me a couple of shots. Swish one, swish two, boy, my game seems to be on, and the females are watching. Fully feeling myself, I decide to dunk on my next attempt and I bogged—everyone began laughing even the females who were watching. I said to them,

"Man, I'm in my school uniform." No one is trying to hear that, they were like, "Boy, you can't jam."

As the day quickly rolled by and school had ended, I began to think about my future during the bus ride home. Looking around and observing the young men in our community, I know I didn't want to be a failure. All I needed was one shot, one shot to prove myself worthy of my existence. Suddenly, sirens rang from afar you could hear that the sound was getting close. The ambulance zoomed by as the vehicle pulled to the side of the road. Being just minutes away from the scene, I can see a person being placed carefully on the stretcher. I whisper softly, "I hope the person be all right." It appeared that it had been a serious car collision involving three vehicles. It's sort of strange how we manage to get in accidents here in Nassau, seeing whereas the roads are so small.

Finally arriving to my destination I shout, "Bus stop!" The driver slowed down and reached out his hands to collect the bus fee. I only had a dollar in which it's only fifty cents for the bus ride, but I told him, "Don't worry about it." When I got home, there was a note on the table saying to fold up clothes in the wash room and clean the dishes in the kitchen. First thing first, let me tackle my homework, and then I'll get over to the dishes. Tumbling through the rubbish in my bag, I stumbled over a few project sheets, which has some close deadline dates. I instantly began to work on those, before I knew it I heard Mom car pulling in the driveway, so I ran over to the kitchen to start washing the dishes because I know just how she goes. Not realizing that the clothes were still in the dryer, Mom came stomping her way through the kitchen and onto the washroom. I totally forgot, but the reminder came with a slap in the back of my head. Stunned by the blow, I immediately turned around with a disgruntle look on my face and said, "I was doing my homework." Mom wasn't hearing that. I guess in some cases, I couldn't blame her because it's been times where I made up excuses for not folding the clothes. Now, finally done washing the dishes, it seems as if Mom was still frustrated. She kept going on and on about how I'm going to be just like my dad. See, Dad left a long time ago, and he was never really in our lives. He's always in and out of jail whether here in Nassau or in Florida, so I guess it's still a bitter feeling inside.

Soaking up the emotions, I quietly made my exit through the front door, taking a deep breath I gently crept up onto the hood of Mom's vehicle and laid back on the windshield. Sitting there for good thirty minutes, I decide to make a wish, with tears running down my cheeks, I began encouraging myself, praying to God that I don't want to be unsuccessful or a jail bird like my dad.

The following day at school, I made a vow just before entering the gates of CC Sweeting High School. There will be no lack in my work ethic. I will make sure everything I do will reflect a person that is respectful and dependable to all my teachers and administrators.

CHAPTER 2

Tryouts for our high school basketball are right around the corner, and I'm looking forward to being in the school team. It's a challenge seeing whereas Mom always dragging me off the court for the smallest reasons, but I have the perfect plan.

The weekend is right there, and I can't wait to get home to ask T if he's going to the court Friday, even though today is only Wednesday. That's my jamming buddy, we've been doing this since we were little kids. He's a really good friend of mine. I must've drifted for a few minutes during class time because Ms. Carey was breathing down my neck with a bunch of questions, but I wasn't paying attention. Luckily, the bell rang for the period to end. "Whoa! That was close," I murmured. Thinking I was scot free, the teacher told me to stay behind for a few minutes because she wanted to speak with me. I wondered what I did wrong, but as she began explaining, I realized it was totally the opposite. She expressed that I need to stay focus during class time and that there was a good possibility I could make the honor role. I don't know if she noticed, but there was an overwhelming joy that came over me. It felt like with every step I was making, it was slow, but surely coming together.

All evening, I thought about what my teacher said, figuring this would be some good news to share with my peeps. A sudden *bam* echoed through the hallways of the house, but it took me a few seconds before I responded to the sound. Running from my bed room to the living room area to see what is going on, I noticed Shana sitting quietly on the couch as if someone told her not to move. I could see the fear in her eyes as her lips whispered, "Mommy and Daddy are in the room rowing." I told her to go to her room and play for a few minutes, just to get her away from the argument. Not to clear on what the altercation is about, but Mom and Tommy never seem to get along, I wondered many times how and why they were together. To be honest, I never had any problems with Tommy, but as far as being a real *father* figure, he never seem to fill that void. When I stop and really think about the years he's been around, I can't remember one single time he went out on the court with me or attended a Parent-teacher Conference, or any of the above. This is where I mainly wish that my father was in my life to share these special moments with him, to have that love and support because it gets very discouraging at times.

With the night coming to a halt, I realized that I had forgotten to ask T if he was jamming on Friday, but I'll have to chat with him tomorrow. Arriving to school early this morning, I see the most beautiful girl in CC Sweeting High School, her name is Jasmine Mills and she's also prefect. "Man, she is gorgeous," I whispered to myself. Building up the nerve to approach, I decided to introduce myself to her.

"Hi, Jasmine, my name is Drexel Robertson, but everyone calls me Dre!"

"Well you already know my name, so have a nice day," She replied.

Embarrassment drains down from ear to ear as I walked to my classroom and for the whole first period of the day. I kept wondering if it was the braces in my mouth, but during break time, I saw her snatch up with this guy we call "Pretty Ricky," it suddenly dawn on me that she's attracted to guys with a bright complexion and curly hair. That evening after school, I decided to save my lunch money so that I could've purchase a small jar of Noxzema and a box of S-curls. Trotting over to T's house, Mom suddenly pulls up alongside me saying, "Where you going, Drexel?"

"I was going right by Tavaren," I replied. She told me to be quick about it because she needs me to get something from out of the shed. Wow! No fuss, I believe Mom really likes Tavaren's character because whenever I mention his name, she would always have a different response—almost to say like he is good in her books. Excited to talk to my boy, I caught myself screaming out his name from the road, expecting him to come to the window, his mother instead looks through the curtains letting me know that he wasn't home as yet. She told me to try back in another hour or so, but all I'm thinking is that I may not be able to come back base on how Mom sounded.

For sure I was right because as soon as I stepped inside the house. she shouts, "Drexel take the gas container from out of the shed and put it in the car for me please."

My first thought is, *Whose vehicle ran out of gas?* But right after I was finish doing what she ask, she also added that after school tomorrow she wants me to lawn the yard. Putting two and two together, I understood the purpose of the gas container—it was because the lawn mower was low on gas. I sucked my teeth for the whole night, mumbling words that didn't make any sense.

Finally, today is Friday, the day I've waiting for, to play some ball, but it's still a bitter sweet feeling though because of a constant reminder that Mom wants me to mow the lawn. "Shucks, man!" I screamed in the middle of our class session. By the time I caught myself, I was already tangled in another humiliating scene. I could hear my classmate chuckling while the teacher asked, "Mr. Robertson, what is your problem?" His voice firm as he waives his hands for the class to be quiet. I guess he figured I was directing the statement to him. Quickly, I apologized and got through the situation safely.

Back at my homework class, the teacher announced that there will be a meeting held after school for anyone that wants to join the Junior Achievement Club. "Yeah that's what I'm talking about!" as I shout loudly throughout the classroom. All the guys agreed that if it's anywhere you want to meet the ladies, this was the ideal spot. Laughing amongst ourselves, a familiar voice made its way across the classroom, it was Jasmine Mills, and boy, she looks even better today. I couldn't stop staring as she conversed with one of my classmates. She eventually turned as all the noise and laughter caught her attention. Quickly, I turned the opposite way because I didn't want her to think I was a pervert, but she must've seen me looking. From the corner of my eyes, I can see her and her friends laughing, pointing their hands in my direction. It seem as if everyone picked up that I have an interest in Jasmine Mills. I think she is a bit flattered by that because she waived and said, "Hi, Dre."

Before I could respond, the bell rang for our last class period. Save by the bell, I figured this would provide me with an opportunity to think about what I want to say when we meet again. I remembered a few years back when I had an interest in this young lady that we used to call "Missy," and I allowed T to act as me during a phone conversation one afternoon.

Suddenly, Missy began calling him, rather than calling me. That was crazy, and I promised myself I would never do that again, so with this particular situation it was all on me. Heading over to the meeting after our last period of classes, guess who I bump into going up the staircase? Jasmine freaking Mills! Apparently, she is signing up too for the club.

At that very moment, it felt like everything was moving in slow motion. I could not get a grip of myself; I think I even stumbled coming up the stairs where I was so nervous. For the whole time that the advisors were giving us details on what JA was about, I just kept staring, wondering what I could say to spark some kind of interest. I knew I had already made a fool of myself for the day, not once, but twice already. She seemed to have it altogether as I watched from a distance. She's smart, she's beautiful, and she is very popular. How could I match up with this? I think I drowned myself so deep in my thoughts that the opportunity came and left within that split second and I never said anything. The journey home was a difficult one. It felt as if someone had knocked the wind out of me, plain and simple, I felt defeated. Even worst, today is Friday, and I'm standing here in the yard prepping to mow the lawn. I could see T coming over in his basketball attire to ask the big question. I even hate to face him right now because I really want to go, especially coming off a day like this. I need to get my frustration out, so I decided to do a section of the yard today and leave the final touches for tomorrow. I told T to give me a couple of minutes to finish up. Of course, he was fine with that because it was still early. It took me at least an additional hour and a half to touch up the front section, so before any more time is consumed, I'm going to stop for now.

Kane just arrived from work, and I shouted, "We're about to head to the court." But from his facial expression it was obvious that he had other plans. Still he replied, "I will catch you guys up."

The distance is quite far, so me and T decided to jog until we were able to see the court, and boy, was it packed? It seem as if everyone is excited to play today. The first team game I got picked, it's me, T, Duran and

Wallace. Wallace is a terror on the boards, and Duran is a straight up hustler. With T handling the ball, I could see this is going to be an awesome night for us.

Boom! We won the first game. Boom! We won the second game.

The third game is a bit intense because the guy I'm matched up with is slightly taller than I am.

T looks at me and says, "Boy, Dre, you know your lip is bleeding right?"

I replied, "No, I didn't notice." But that wasn't stopping me from playing, we were down thirteen to seven, and the game is going to fifteen. Wallace kept us in the game. He was hitting shots from every angle of the court while Duran was dominating on the defensive end. Now here it is, the score is fourteen to thirteen, we're still down and we need one to tie and two to win the game. "T" suddenly makes a nice drive to the bucket to tie the score; it's now our big chance to win the game. Wallace brings the ball inbound to T, "T" then pass the ball back to Wallace for an isolation play, we all spread the court to allow him to go work on this guy, but as Wallace was making his move to the bucket, the big guy who was guarding me slipped over to double team Wallace. Wallace saw me open in the corner and passed the ball to me for the open shot. I positioned myself to take the game winning shot, but out of the blue, the big guy who was guarding me came flying out of nowhere and blocks the ball. His teammate quickly grabbed the loose ball and tossed it right back to him for the game winning point. We lost, and Wallace surely made that clear, he kept saying, "You were open, Dre, you were open." I looked at T to see his response, he looked back at me I guess to see if I had anything to say, but I didn't. While gathering up our items to leave, T said, "Bro, don't worry about it. We won the first two games."

Once he said that, it was good enough for me because instead of looking at the game we lost. He made me look at the games we won, and I think that was a valuable lesson I learned. Tonight is a full moon and it's very humid, I can't wait to get in the shower. I'm really exhausted and my feet are killing me. I even have blisters in my hands. It just hit me that maybe when I was mowing the lawn that this may have occurred, but at that moment, I was so excited, I didn't pay it no mind.

Wow, it's morning already, with the sun beaming down on my bed head, I can feel the aches and pains from yesterday. The house is somewhat quiet other than the noise coming from the early morning shows Shana's watching, even though today is Saturday, Mom is still schedule to work, and Tommy has been gone from 5:30 a.m. for his regular bus route, so it's only me and Shana.

Hmm, now what chores can I give Shana to do, I'm thinking to myself. I'm in charge now, and she can't do a damn thing about it. Well, the bathroom needs some tidying, and these rugs are very dusty. Oh! The clothes have to fold also because I never got a chance to complete those. With a sturdy voice, I said to Shana, "You need to clean up before you could sit and watch television." One thing I must admit, Shana may have complained, but she surely got the work done.

Suddenly, a knock at the door, Shana answers, "Who is it?" The person replied, "This is Kane." I could hear from my bedroom that it was Kane's voice, so I allowed him to wait for a few minutes intentionally, by the time as I got there he was gone. I stepped out on the car patio to see if I could catch him trotting home, but when I looked around, he wasn't nowhere in sight. On my way back inside, I heard laughter coming from T's house. I decided to see what was going on. So as I'm getting closer to door, I can hear Kane's voice and at the same time T is continuously laughing his head off, so I took it upon myself and open the door screaming, "What's up, bitches!"

Kano politely turns around saying, "Yeah, lazy boy, I heard you stink up the court last night." I just ignored him because I know T isn't that kind of person to just sit and talk behind your back. In fact, Kane always has a smart remark, "Like you dead as crap." Especially when it comes to playing ball, but it's cool because when we go out today I'm going to show him who's really dead.

Jeers were being thrown back and forth for the whole time that we're there, so we decided that we'll just settle it this afternoon. "T" wasn't even toning into us, he was busy playing his video game with his brother, Vano. I simply just eased my way out saying, "I have to check on Shana because she's home by herself." I just remembered my cousin, Carlos, supposed to be passing through today, but I'm not too interested in him and the tribe coming this way because they love to eat everything they see especially when we have the shop open, but perhaps the flipside to that is they could probably keep Shana's company, while me and Carlos go out to the basketball court. "Yeah that sound like a plan," I whisper to myself. Just as I figure, about an hour and some in to the afternoon, my aunt and five out of her nine kids came strolling in, but only my two youngest cousins along with Carlos decided to stay. They brought their dolls and some hair products to play with, so I didn't mind because this will definitely keep them busy for the time being. Before we left to go, I told Shana that we were going right around the corner for a while, I also added that she must make sure keep the door lock, and if Mom calls while we're out, to let her know that we were with T. Carlos is a pain in the butt, he believes that he's better than me at everything, so when it comes to basketball, he think he's the next *Michael Jordan*, I schooled him from every angle of the court.

Aw, boy! Here comes Kane, Demetrio, and T, now it's on, the only thing is that they will have to wait until this game is finish. I could hear Kane from the side lines screaming, "I'm gonna dunk on ya' head today!" Today seem to be a better shooting day for me because most of my buckets were coming from the perimeter. I just love the height advantage I have over these guys. I know the next team game I'm going to have to change up the game plan seeing whereas Kane matches up pretty well against me. I picked up Carlos on my team to even off the numbers, but I can't have him playing defense on T because my boy is lightning fast, and I'll have to switch off Kane to help Carlos. I'm screaming to the top of my voice, "Man, we're getting murder out here. Okay, Carlos, you switch over to Demetrio and I'll guard T, we'll let Nado lock down on Kane," I further exclaim. "We look like we working out a little better," saying softly as we played.

Peep, peep, peep as a horn sounded, T shouts, "Dre, that looks like your mother."

"Yeah, bro, that's Betsy." Carlos says in a timid voice. We both dashed over to the vehicle, I could see from the look on her face that whatever it is, it isn't good.

"Drexel, get your black ass in this car," Mom shouted with her face screwed up. I didn't even see when Carlos jump into the vehicle, I met him slump down in the back seat with his eyes locked outside the back glass. Everything felt like it was moving in slow motion for the whole ride home. Mom is really fired up as her hands waive from left to right and her mouth spilling out the meanness words that you only could imagine. As I looked into the rear view mirror, I could see Carlos breathe a sigh of relief when he saw his mother's vehicle parked in the front of the yard. Apparently, they were on their way out, but I don't think it was because they were ready to go. I think my aunt understood that Mom is frustrated. Today, it's worn heavy on Mom's face, and I'm honestly afraid of what she is going to do. Instantly after my aunt left, Mom lets it all out, and every piece of object that she found, it was being laid across my body. *I can't believe she is hitting me like this*, is all that's running through my mind. "Ah, ah, ah," I screamed and shouted. "Mommy, Mommy, please!" I continue screaming. "Shut up!" Mom shouted. "You must be thinking I do play," she went on saying.

Finally, she stops as Tommy crept through the door. Tommy doesn't say a word and Mom just turns her head, walking into the kitchen as if nothing had just happened. I'm left picking up the torn pieces from my sweaty T-shirt. I limp gently into the bathroom to collect my thoughts and sat quietly on the toilet seat. I feel like tearing myself out of my skin, I feel so disgusting and ugly. Maybe I am worthless, and I don't know my ass from my elbow, like my mother said. Moments after taking a long shower, I decided to sneak the cordless phone into the bedroom to make a call. With each digit that I attempt to press, I trembled. The first attempt, I hung up, and then I tried once again. Surprisingly, the call went through, which is very rare because every time I call, it gives a busy signal.

The grungy voice shouts, "Hello!" I reply with a solemn voice, "Hey, Dad, how's it going?" With a brief pause he says, "Who this?"

"Daddy, this is me Drexel." It is quite obvious that he is surprise because he began laughing sporadically saying, "Boy, when you coming to visit your Daddy, because you know I have a room waiting for you?"

I told him as soon as school close for the summer. We laugh and talk for a good twenty minutes into the night. It feels real nice hearing his voice and as I'm about to say, "I miss you, Daddy."

He utters the words, "I miss you, son, and I love you."

I immediately replied, "I miss you too, Dad, and I will always love you, regardless." He must've sense from the way I sounded that it was more I wanted to express, so I began to tell him what Mom been doing to me, but he kept saying, "Don't worry, when you become eighteen, you can move in with me. You'll be of age then," he further exclaim.

After our conversation, I felt somewhat comforted by what he told me, but at the same time, the reality is I would still have to endure through this situation—being in a house with what appears to be strangers.

CHAPTER 3

Channeling my energy in a more positive perspective, I began working diligently day in and day out, ticking off every subject with at least a (B) average, and thanks to Ms. Gomez, my hospitality teacher, I'm beginning to develop a great relationship with the other teachers on the campus. Everyone thinks that I'm a suck up, but I don't care because when a man is push to his limits, he has to do some unusual stuff in order to make things happen. So far for the year, I have participated in "It's Academics," and won two Spelling B Competitions, and from the basketball tryouts, things are looking pretty good, but Mom still isn't allowing me to go out on the court, so only at school I'm able to practice. With the end of term exams coming up, it's probably best that I don't bother with that any way.

The scent of a sizzling fried fish leaks through the cracks of the door way, it draws me away from my studies. Slowly, I'm being led by the aroma, and as I'm going toward the kitchen, I stop to look at Mom as she slice and dice the herbs on the counter. For a brief moment, I began to think to myself that she looks so peaceful and that she can't hurt a fly, but within a quick flash, I know exactly what's stored up on the inside. Breaking into a conversation, I tried explaining to Mom that I was trying out for the basketball team this year. She says instantly, "Well, I don't know what for because basketball can't get you far. What about your school work?" she firmly stated.

Filled with excitement, I express how well my grades were looking, and that I was Student of the Month, just recently. She didn't utter a word, but I didn't let it bother me none. In fact, I will prove it to her on report card day. Continuing on with my studies, the phone rings and it just rang and rang as if nobody wanted to answer, so I aggressively picked up the phone saying, "Hello."

A gentle and calm voice replies, "Well, hello, Dre. How my favorite nephew doing?" Right away, I knew who it was because it's only one person that calls hear with this meek voice. Calmly I say, "Hi, Aunt Mary."

"Boy, how you know this ya Aunt Mary? Anyway what happen to ya'll phone?"

I replied, "Man, sorry about that, Aunt Mary, I think everyone is busy because Mom is in the kitchen cooking, and I'm in my room studying."

"Well that is what I love to hear," she said.

"Child, Drexel, you have to stay focus in school," she further exclaims.

"Yeah I know, Auntie, but at times it feels so difficult—"

As I'm about to continue on, she interrupts and says, "Remember all things are possible through Christ Jesus who strengthens us." I grin to myself and told her, "I know."

"Anyway, your Auntie love you and we'll chat later, let me say a quick word to Betsy," she said.

After handing the phone to Mom, I couldn't stop smiling at Aunt Mary, she always seem to be in such high spirit and always has encouraging words on the tip of her tongue. Just as I'm about to settle back in my room, Tommy came banging on my door saying that Tavaren is outside, to me I wondered what was it about because as far as I'm concerned, it's a bit late to go out on the court, in fact, I can't go even if I wanted too.

"Hay, midget," is my first response.

"Dude, I still growing," He uttered.

I couldn't help but laugh because he's been this height from the day I first met him.

"Listen," he said.

"On a serious note, I need a favor from you, dude."

I'm like, "What you need, bro?"

Now I'm thinking to myself, *He's in trouble with his girlfriend and needs me to lie for him.* But instead, he tells me that he's going to need me to sign this form stating that he is putting in his hours for community service. For graduation, this is one of the criteria's you need to have before graduating from High School. I place my hand under my chin saying, "So who I'm pretending to be?"

"Well you're one of the members from church," he murmurs.

"Now make sure you sign your own name, so it doesn't be any mix up when they decide to call," he continued saying.

I'm like, "Cool, no problem, dude!"

As he walks off, he kept screaming, "Now, don't forget, Drexel. Don't forget!"

Mmm! Smells like the food is finally done, so I'm going to wrap it up for the night and continue my studies tomorrow. While taking up my food, the funniest thing occurred, Shana was apparently watching a sitcom earlier today that showed the family members all seated at the dining room table eating and she ask Mom, "Why we don't eat at the table like a family?" Mom was shock and totally blew by that question as if nothing was said. I politely mumble under my breath, "Because this is a dysfunctional family." I don't think Shana fully understands that Tommy isn't my biological father and I just happen to live here with them.

Evening upon evening, I'm hit with chores; Mom became more and more relentless. The only good thing is that this week will be the final pick for the basketball team. I know I'm better than most of the guys so that is a no brainer; I just hope I land a starting position on the team. The weather is suddenly changing, so I decided to wear my jacket today at school. These days are listed to be the season you get snatch up with your girlfriend, but unfortunately, I don't have any. It seems as if all the girls I am interested in are not interested in me, especially Jasmine. I'm using that Noxzema every day, and that S-curls have my hair wavy as hell, but it's only attracting the chicken-head girls.

During break time, I stumble into Coach Barry he said, "The team will be having a meeting right after school." I replied in a high pitch voice, "Okay, sir, I'll be there!" The minute I turned my back to head over to the tuck shop, two twelfth-graders came storming down the corridor. It seems as if one is carrying a knife in his hand. I'm not sure, but before I knew it, the whole school was running toward the back of the school yard including myself. There were rocks being thrown from left to right. I'm suddenly ducking and dodging—not understanding the reason why.

I can hear vaguely one of our administrators screaming over the PA system, "All students report to your homeroom class, now." I manage to get back to my classroom safely, but it appears that a few of the students got injured. In a matter of seconds, there were police vehicles and an ambulance swarming the scene. Looking over the crowd, I can see policemen escorting five of our students into their cars; this isn't something new for us because with the Bain Town crew, it's like a jungle in this place.

Emotions were running wild throughout the rest of the day. Our last period, which was English language, didn't feel like a classroom setting because Mr. Rolle was basically in and out during the whole period. After classes were done, I made my way to the basketball court for the meeting. Looking around, the group seems to be small in numbers, but after about twenty minutes of just waiting, one of the guys came jogging to the back with an update from coach.

"Coach Barry said the meeting will be postpone today because he had to go down by the station," he said.

I said brazenly, "Until when?"

The guy was not sure, so he just shrugged his shoulders as to say he didn't know. "What a day," I quietly said walking to the bus terminals. Look at these students, they are like wild animals. I can't even get on a bus without being push to the side. I want tell this dude so bad that he just stepped on my shoes, but I know exactly where that will lead, and I don't want any problems. I know half of these dudes have way more issues that I do at home, speaking about home, here comes the twins, Mon and Ron.

As I make my exit off the bus, Mon shouts, "Look here, Dre, lend your boy an ace." I knew once I gave him this, I wasn't going to get it back, and as I reached down into my pocket to feel for how much money I had, Ron suddenly says, "Bro, I need an ace too."

I replied, "Ya'll think I'm an ATM machine ay?" Both of them began chuckling in this wicked tone that they normally do when they're up to no good. Everyone on our block knew the twins were like sly fox. I only had a dollar and fifty left, so I just gave them what I had and kept moving right along. It's funny how everyone has this concept that we are rich, but I think if we were truly rich, we wouldn't be in this neighborhood. Kane especially, always saying I was born with a silver spoon in my mouth, but that isn't the case. I believe that Mom just know how to work with the little she has. For example, the store she placed onto the house, and honestly, I hate it because I usually have to manage it all the time. In fact, this money isn't even for me, this is going toward Shana's school fund. I'm graduating within the next year, and I'm thinking, *What about me?*

Sitting on the edge of my bed, going through my school work, I begin to rub my eyes from the tiresome day. The evening is soothing and the air is fresh, with just two deep breaths, I fell right off to sleep. It's nearing the end of the hurricane season, so the weather is still off and on. Mom is yelling, "Let's go." Because the rain is coming down harder and harder, it's really difficult trying to get somewhere on time especially when the weather is like this the traffic is thick. I'm sure Mom got to work late this morning because I got to school shortly after nine o'clock and she hasn't drop Shana as yet.

For a good portion of the day, my mind was set on if we would have the meeting with Coach Barry, so to calm my nerves, I took it upon myself to go over to the PE department to find out some information. He yelled, "Oh yeah, we'll meet right after school."

Excited about the response I got from Coach Barry, I went smiling back to my class and everyone is like, "Dude, what are you so happy about?" I think I didn't know either because for every person that asks, I had a different answer. By the end of the day, the sun had come out solid, now it's extremely hot. Just about everyone in the classroom is holding a book to fan with.

Uncomfortable is how I'm feeling right about now, so I decided to raise my hand to get my teacher's attention. I asked if I could be excuse to go the restroom, and she happily oblige saying yes. I took my time walking along the corridor as I embraced some of the cool air, it wasn't much difference, but it was better than being in the classroom.

No matter what time of day it is, you always have a group of guys that are trying to duck classes, and guess where the overrated spot is? In the restroom. Wow! I don't even want to use the restroom anymore, so I damp my hands with some cold water and pat it over my face for a quick cool off. Checking my watch, I realized it's only a few more minutes left before the bell rings for classes to be dismissed, and on my way going into the classroom almost simultaneously the same boys that were hiding in the bathroom were being escorted to the office by the vice principal. I was in awe as I sat to my desk, just barely missing his roundabout, he usually does this particular hour, even though I wasn't with them, it probably still wouldn't have made a difference because it is normal for student to make up excuses of why they're not in their classrooms. The bell just rang a few minutes ago, and I'm caught trying to quickly scribble down my assignment from off the chalk board. I don't want to be late for the meeting, so dashing through the corridor, I made it just in time before they got started. Shockingly, this time all the guys were there, so Coach Barry got right to it. After doing his evaluation, and letting each individual know that this team was, the toughest group he's ever had to pick.

He sighs then says, "All the names I call, stand beside me." We all stood there waiting in anticipation for our names to be called. Randy Smith, Elliott Bain, Kendall Jennings, Baron Taylor, and after exactly ten more names that were called, he finally call mine. Placing the word *and* in the front of my name, making it known I was the final name on the list. Here I stand alongside the fourteen guys whose names were called, with a smirk on my face trying my best not to laugh,

Coach Barry gently rolls the sheet he has in his hand and clears his throat saying, "All the guys whose name I didn't call, report to practice here tomorrow afternoon." Completely confused, everything inside me suddenly dropped, I could not believe my ears. Coach Barry then turns toward us with this calm look that he usually has, "Guys, I don't want ya'll to be discouraged because it really was a tough decision, but you will not be on this year's team."

All that's running through my mind is, *Yeah, right. Whatever, dude. You already showed favoritism.*

But I held my composure, only up until I got home. The minute I placed my hands on my room door to swing it open, I burst into tears thinking that maybe Mom was right about basketball—that it wouldn't get me far. Even the neighborhood thinks I'm not going to make it anywhere in basketball, and now to help confirm that fact, I was cut from my high school basketball team.

CHAPTER 4

Rapidly, I watch as the seasons past, and I'm constantly reminded of that day—that day I was cut from the team. Me, T, and Vano are just chilling at the back patio grilling, having some good old laughs, and T happens to mention that he's deciding to quit his basketball team. I'm like, "What, why dude?"

Smoothly launching off in the chair he utters, "Well, I want to concentrate more on my academics."

Having thoughts of, *Yeah that sounds awesome*! But still envying him because of my own situation, I manage to squeeze out, "Yeah, bro, I agree!"

"Where do you see yourself in another five years, bro?" extending the conversation.

This question must've really interest him because he sits up saying in a firm tone, "Owning my business."

I simply reply, "Well don't procrastinate because time waits on no man."

From the shadows of where I'm standing, Vano shouts, "Boy, you like to use that word *nah*."

I turned around from taking the meat off the grill with a slight grin off my face, T looks at me smiling then we paused for a split second and we all just burst into laughing.

"Anyone ready for another burnt hotdog?" shouting as I held the fork up in the air.

As the evening slowly progresses, we're stuff to capacity that when it came time to clean up the scrapings from around the yard, it was a struggle, but we knew Mom was going to be home shortly and we didn't want any problems. Something must've popped in Vano's head because after we were done clearing the scene, out of left field he utters, "Bro?" and I'm like, "What happen?" With no hesitation he replies, "We forgot to grill the steaks we had in the freezer." I couldn't contain myself as once again I was dying from laughter because as far as we were concerned, both the chickens and the hotdogs were more than enough. Still not acknowledging that we were totally cracking on him he boldly says, "Anyway, same time tomorrow." After everything was settled, I found myself standing in the mirror while placing a bit of Noxzema on my face asking the same question, "Where do I see myself in another five years?"

Gently washing the Noxzema from my cheeks as the water drips from my chin, I stood firmly looking deep into my own eyes saying, "I'm not going to be a jail bird like my dad." Especially after receiving information later on from my stepmother that he was involved in another situation, which was a *third strike*. I heard that the laws in the United States are really strict, so once he had committed another offence, he would be thrown in jail for good.

Not a day goes by that I don't think about if he was around because maybe I would've made the basketball team or maybe Mom would've treated me different. It really hurts knowing the reality of some situations because on one hand, Mom isn't interested in my dreams, and on the other hand, my dad is incarcerated. Mom is still shocked that I'm doing so well in school. I looked at her face based on the last report, she was totally in disbelief. Finally, after hours of just tossing and turning in my bed, I'm able to relax in a comfortable position and go off to sleep.

Feeling like the night was cut short, I'm awakened by a loud horn coming directly from outside the yard. Shana screams, "Drexel, that's the church bus." Grumpy and discombobulated, I instantly said, "Well tell them we aren't going this morning." But apparently, Shana was up from early because she was already dress and ready to go. As I look on, she grabs her little purse and says politely, "See you later because I can't be late for Sunday school." I guess I'm not the only one around here that is full of surprises. Before I could utter another word, the door slams and everything goes back silent. *Who in the world is this character?* I thought to myself. She even manages to fix herself a little breakfast. I'm not washing any dishes though.

Wondering around in the kitchen, I'm like a lost puppy, so I decided to go over by Kane's for something to eat, but instead they were like, "Dude, we were coming over by you." Rubbing the cold from eyes, I said, "Let's see what T saying." Instead, we met T and Vano getting ready for church. With no regard for his tongue,

Vano shouts, "Ya'll dudes, need to get ready for church!" "Man can't live by bread alone ya' know!" he further exclaims. Staring across the street, the traffic begins to build up as the cars park along the grass outside T's yard, sucking his teeth Kane murmurs, "These people like to park in front of ya' yard nah." Feeling guilty as they prep to leave, I told Kane I'm going to dash home real quick and throw on something. The positive thing about this situation is that we live right opposite the church. "Give me ten minutes guys," I shouted.

Flipping through the closet, I murmur to myself, "Okay, what do I have here.

Yeah, this suit looks like it could work." I just remember I showered up last night, so I don't have to bathe, I could just wash my face and brush my teeth. As I'm locking the door, I can hear Vano shouting from the road.

"Where the hell you going dress like that?"

I simply said, "Don't be mad at a real dresser. Besides, I might meet Mrs. Robertson in there," I added.

Scratching the back of his head Kane steps in and says, "Dude, please, nobody want you, especially looking like that."

T was already on the inside, so we all just slid alongside him as we filled the row. Looking at T, I can see just a slight smirk on his face, but he's trying his hardest not to laugh at what I was wearing. I believe we were all seeking out the sexiest females in the building. Kane gives me a nudge, "Check out the girl to my right," He says. I look back at him and grin. During the whole worship period, I was in gulp in a full conversation with

Vano. He loves to laugh and I love to crack jokes, so it's a perfect combination. It must've been noticeable because shortly after one of the ushers gave me a signal as to say stop what we were doing. I politely tap Kane and told him the ushers were trying to get his attention.

The church is full to its capacity, and the energy is high voltage—persons are jumping around screaming to the top of their voices. I back off a bit to allow this one young lady to do her thing because it was like she got strike by lightning, and I didn't want to get in the way of that.

Moments of just standing there, I look down to glance at my watch, my eyes become weary.

Suddenly, I felt a blow that struck at the back of my head. "Open your eyes, bro, the pastor is about to come on," T boldly stated.

"Bro, you had to hit me to tell me that," is my initial response. But I don't say nothing and as he's about to open his mouth to utter a response to my reaction, a voice shouts, "Let us pray." Everything went silent. The whole congregation has their heads bow, the only thing that you can hear are the fans spinning and a raspy voice praying. Words of *yes Lord* are whispered throughout the church, and as the pastor nears the end of the prayer, he firmly says, "And let the church say. Amen."

I glimpse to see what T is doing, but he is more attentive than I usually am in the classroom. Kane still has his head bow and his eyes closed as if the prayer is still going on. Vano is fiddling with a piece of thread hanging from his pants pocket. Placing my back gently against the bench, I begin to hear these words that penetrate my spirit, "Living a purpose-filled Life."

I'm not sure if it's the tone or the theme that captures my attention, but I'm suddenly rocked by this man's message, and I'm all down his throat listening to every word that is spoken. My eyes become glassy. I rub them adding a yawn to make it appear like I'm still tired from the early morning disturbance. I didn't bother to look to my right nor to my left because I felt like I would have broken into tears from the powerful message and as the beautiful sound of music softly stream along the walls of the church, the pastor begins to bring his message to a close.

Persons in the congregation started to make their way to the altar as he humbly says, "Before I close today, if there is anyone that needs a special prayer or would love to accept the Lord as their personal Savior, I want you to come forward and allow us to pray with you."

I can feel the electricity flowing through my body as my spirit begins to rise, but my physical body doesn't respond. Suddenly, Kane knocks me with his elbow saying, "Let's go, bro, while everyone is moving." T probably figured it was a good time to leave also because he followed right behind as we made are exit. All of us went our separate ways to our destination. With no words being exchange or no jokes to laugh at, it became just a quiet walk home. In my mind, I wondered if any of them felt the same way I did, but I did not dare ask because most of the things I was experiencing I never expressed—it just wasn't a cool thing to do. Dusting my feet on the carpet as I scrabble through my pocket for my house keys, I can hear the cries coming from inside the church. It's an uncomfortable feeling entering the house knowing that could've possibly been me in that position. Throwing my jacket across the dining room chair, I further understood that Shana hadn't arrived as yet. Gracefully, I began stripping bit by bit until I reached my bedroom, I clipped on the air condition and dove straight into bed.

After being asleep for about two hours, I got up feeling slightly rested. Managing to drag myself to the front room area, I noticed that Shana is nowhere to be found, the TV is on, but no Shana. "Shucks where the hell this girl is?" I murmured. Getting a bit paranoid, I began shouting her name throughout the house, but still no answer. I decided to put on my slippers to see if she would be outside in the yard somewhere, but instead I run into Simone, Simone is one of kind, she lives right in the back of T, but she carries herself like she owns the neighborhood. Here she comes walking along the street, so I took it upon myself to ask her where she was going because if my memory serves me correctly, she is only four-years-old.

Boldly, she looks up at me and says, "I going by my Auntie."

Quickly responding I say, "By yourself?"

Politely, she answers, "Yes, sir."

All I'm thinking is, *Where the hell is this young lady's peeps* and on second thought *Why isn't her older sister with her?* Simone continues along her path as I stood there shaking my head, but at the same time I'm thinking I have my own situation to tend too. Here I am screaming through the neighborhood and just as I'm about to scream her name once again, her and DD (Simone's older sister) come strolling right along. The crazy thing about the whole situation is that she walks right pass me as if I wasn't standing there.

Annoyed, I yanked her by the arm and said, "Don't you ever leave the house without telling me, you hear me?" I looked at her face and saw how terrified she was. It reminded me of whenever Mom would grab me and give me a piece of her mind. I don't want her to think that I would bring any harm to her or that I don't love her, but she has to understand that I was worried and if anything was to ever happen to her, I wouldn't be able to live with myself.

Fact is, I never got a chance to express that with her, but she surely remembered to express with Mom and Tommy when they got home as Mom is wilding out and screaming to the top of her lungs. Tommy has this serious look like he wants to do something. I tried to explain, but nobody wants to hear my side of the story they just figured whatever it was, that it was my fault in any event. Mom tops it off by saying I didn't know my ass from my elbow and from the look on Tommy's face, it seem as if he totally concurs. After they were done damaging every aspect of my character, I just quietly walked off to my bedroom and went off to sleep.

CHAPTER 5

Summer is quickly approaching, and the students are wilding out. The twelfth graders are preparing for graduation, so they don't have much on their minds. It's this one particular dude who's always in trouble and knowing most of the staff, I know they can't wait for him to leave. Taking a quick scan through this year's graduated class, it seems to be a very small amount that will be walking away with their diploma. Most of them spent their year in and out of the classroom because of some fight they were involved in. It makes me somewhat appreciate the home I come from even though it's dysfunctional, but for most of these guys dysfunctional is an understatement. Sometimes, I'm surprise of myself of how far I made it.

I can't wait to start the twelfth grade. I think the teachers are even winding down because I'm seated here in my family life class and Ms. Tucker has yet to arrive. Everyone in the classroom is just doing their own thing, and before I realized it, I was caught up in a full conversation with Jacqueline Baptiste. Now I've never really paid her any attention during the whole school year, but it seems like she is a very interesting person, not to mention she has a nice body also, but she isn't so pretty in the face.

It appears that she is very much interested because before I could ask her another question, she whispers, "What's your number, if you don't mind me asking?" It isn't cool for a guy to blush, but I couldn't contain myself as I wrote the number, jokingly I said, "Nah, don't mind the old grumpy person that answers the phone that's my grandmother, she's staying with us for a while."

Amazingly, she couldn't stop laughing. Right away, I knew I'd score. With a slight blush from her she said, "I don't mind because I have one of those at home also."

Really, I was speaking about my mom, but I didn't bother to explain. I simply embraced the moment and laughed right along with her. Suddenly, everyone began scrabbling to get to their desks as Ms. Tucker makes her way to the classroom. I'm already seated, so I politely turned my head to the front and quietly await her arrival.

"Why are you guys standing in my class?" Ms. Tucker shouts with a funny accent onto her voice. No one can really understand her when she speaks, so the whole class chuckles as she stomps her way to her desk. The chuckles only lasted for a second because right after she got up from her desk, she explained that the final exam grades were poor.

Calling each individual up to the front for their exam papers, some began sucking their teeth while others were rolling their eyes. I guess the grades really were horrible base on the reaction from my classmates. Taking a deep sigh as Ms. Tucker calls my name, she extends her hand out toward me with the exam paper hanging down. I'm trying to identify the grade marked on the sheet as I make my way to the front, but I can't make it out. Reaching my hand forward to grab the papers, she looks me dead in the eyes and say, "Excellent job, Mr. Robertson!" she further exclaim that I had the top grade in the class. Blushing once again, I slowly crept back to my desk. Jacqueline pats me on the shoulder and whispers, "Great job." I in turn asked what she got, with a bit of a hesitation she replies, "I got a B."

To my knowledge I know she's pretty smart also because all year she's been averaging a three point and above. *Mmm,* is what I'm thinking to myself, to further push this situation to the next level, our teacher told us that for today's lesson we'll be pairing up into groups, so everyone had to choose a partner. Right away, both I and Jacqueline agreed that we'll partner up. I could sense that she is excited because she can't stop grinning, and I'm looking at her hands as she's writing today's date, her fingers are just trembling. "Wow," I whispered.

She looks up as she taps the pen on her book and gives me the eye saying, "What you say?" Wondering if she really heard me, I took my chances and said, "Oh, I didn't say anything."

All that's running through my mind is, *Calm down, Dre, don't freak ya' self out. You got this.* After the teacher was done handing out the assignment, we got right to work, the topic is, "Single Parents' Homes" and the assignment is to list ten ways society is affected by it. We went back and forth on the topic, it seem as if she also has a lot of issues at home because she mention that her dad doesn't live home with them and that he's married to another woman. I don't discriminate; I just nod my head agreeing to everything she says.

Moments after, the bell rings. But just before leaving, Ms. Tucker makes it clear that the work must be completed for our next meeting. Perfect, now I definitely have a reason to call her tonight. Not allowing her to see the expression on my face, I quickly glanced over to where she and her friends were standing then I gave her the *I'll call you* sign. She smiles saying, "I'll be waiting."

Excited about getting home this evening, I ran into Leonardo Ferguson—he just moved in the area near Parrots Gardens—it's still a good distance from my house, but we started catching the bus together after realizing we were going in the same direction; plus, he's a baller, so he could hang. Just before going straight home, we decided to stop to the tennis store along the way to check out the new stock. Nard said he needed a new pair of tennis for the summer because he wants to play in this year's tournament that we usually host on our court. Where I've been so far out of touch with what's going on in the community, I didn't realize that it was soon near, but I played right along saying, "Yeah, bro, I'm going to be right there killing dudes." Even him and all was like, "Please, Dre, you so dead." I stood straight up bumping my shoulders against his firmly saying, "I'll dunk on your head, bro!" He pushes me off and replies, "Come out tonight and we'll see who'll get dunked on." Knowing my situation, I quickly fire back with, "Well tonight I'm going to be sort of busy."

He just laughed as we boarded the bus to head home. "Shucks, man," I murmured to myself.

From a distance I could see the twins hanging around the bus stop area and I know they're going to definitely bother with me, so instead I allowed the bus driver to pass my stop and I got off with Nard at his stop. He was a bit confused, but I told him I was passing by another friend in the neighborhood. "Later, bro," I shouted as I threw my bag on my back. "Yeah, later," Nard replied.

Wiping my forehead, I suddenly realize the distance I had to walk, I shook my head in regret of getting off the bus with Nard because while he probably was home settled having a meal, I was still out here in the scorching sun.

"Okay, I'm almost there," I said trying to coast myself along the way, but eventually that only lasted for so long, before I could bank the next corner, good the twins and their cousin Tiny came strolling right in my direction. I can hear the wicked grin from where I'm standing and as I approach Ron shouts, "Wha you saying, Dre?" Totally irritated I uttered, "Een nothing."

I quickly tried to slide on by, then Mon steps in saying, "Where you just coming from?" Thinking sharp I replied, "I just came from by your girl, she didn't tell you?" Tiny began laughing as if it was the joke of the year. Ron looked at Mon saying, "Well check out, Drexel." I could tell Mon felt insulted because his face totally turned upside down, but I guess where Tiny was in a rush to catch up with this guy around the corner, they bypass the whole situation and went walking off.

Finally, hitting the street I live on, I slowly took my backpack from off my shoulder and held it in my hand. Passing the park, I see this light-skin girl sitting on the bench. I'm straining my eyes to see exactly who she is and as my vision became clearer, I realize it's only Canova. Canova is a very strange person, so at times she can come off a bit stuck up, but I'll still give it a shot any way. "Hi, sexy, how you doing?" screaming as I stroll on by. And just as I figured she rolls her eyes and turns her head the opposite way. I politely blew a kiss right back at her making her understand that it didn't bother me none because I intentionally did that.

Scratching my head as I open the gate to the yard, I see Tommy's bus park across the street in the church parking lot. Wondering why he's home so early today, I slowly unlocked the door and opened gently, but with the screeching sound, it made it very difficult to enter without being heard. I went straight to my room to take off the sweaty uniform, and while walking out to go into the kitchen, I hear a noise coming from the back of the yard. I look to see what was going on and it was Tommy doing some crap on the patio. It's quite obvious he doesn't know I'm here, so I don't bother to alarm him, I just went around to each room making sure it wasn't any surprises. Honestly, I don't trust Tommy, he's a type of person that doesn't say much, so it's hard to channel into his character. Watching the clock carefully all evening, I'm trying my best not to come off creepy. Anxiously, I anticipate every time the phone rings, that Shana will scream out. The phone is for me, but the whole night goes by and I don't receive one single call.

"Drexel, Drexel, get up, what wrong with you, boy?" Mom shouts. I'm wrapped so deep in sleep I could barely respond, "Uhh, what time is it?" Mom hits me at my back and says, "It's time to get up, it's quarter to seven." Still groggy, I manage to stumble my way to the bathroom. Mom is surprisingly screaming at Shana right now for spilling the tea on the floor, but I instantly make my shower brief because I know at any moment the energy from Mom can shift over in my direction. Just as I'm about to put on my worn-out uniform shirt, here's Shana screaming, "Drexel, telephone!" Curious to know who's on the next line, I rush over to the phone saying, "Hello! Hello!" This deep voice replies, "Drexel, anyone called you from my school as yet?" Picking up on the tone of the voice I realized it was only T.

"No, dude," I murmured with this disgruntle sound in my voice. "Okay, well let me know when they call," he said. Disappointed, I quickly snapped back into reality as Mom once again screams out, "Let's go!"

Arriving minutes after the bell rang; I walked smoothly over to my desk. I look over to see if Jacqueline would say anything, but she doesn't. It's as if we never had a conversation yesterday, and I'm somewhat confuse, but I try to remain as calm as possible not allowing it to show. After pondering the situation, I decided that I'll check myself to make sure it doesn't have anything to do with my physical apparel, so I placed the palm of my hands inches away from my face breathing into it to make sure my breath wasn't tainted. I smell my shirt to make sure it didn't have a musty scent and from my perspective everything seems to be fine.

First period is about to begin, and we're making our way over to the math class, Jacqueline brushes up alongside me and says, "Why you didn't call me?"

Before I could respond she utters, "I did something wrong ay?"

Stuttering, I manage to squeeze out, "No, I was waiting for you to call."

Rolling her eyes, she answers, "You signal to me yesterday that you would call me later."

Thinking about it now, I did say I was going to call her, but I totally forgot. She stood there for a moment just waiting for an answer, but honestly, I'm lost for words.

She shrugs her shoulder and says, "Anyway, don't worry about it, I understand."

As I go to reach out for her hand, Mr. Deal walks up behind me saying, "Mr. Robertson, hurry and get to class."

Seated all the way on the opposite side of the classroom, I ponder to myself, *What could I say to her because I know she feels like I'm not interested.* I try to make eye contact, but she stays focus on the teacher. I think she's ignoring me because I see her face slightly turn as if she knows that I'm trying to get her attention. "Mr. Robertson, can you please hand out the test folders," he calmly said. I jumped up quickly sorting through the pile to find Jacqueline's folder, when I finally got to her papers, I went over to her desk and gently rest the folder in her hands, softly saying, "I want to talk to you at break time."

Of course she didn't answer, but I remained calm. Our next period, we ended up splitting for the option classes; it was cool because I figure it'll give her some time to think.

"Hay, Dre, you know Key Club having a party this weekend right?" Tiffany shouted from behind me.

I looked over my shoulder and replied, "Aw, yeah, where?" Acting as if I'm curious to know, she quickly feeds into to what I said and utters, "Yeah, it's going to be right at Worker's House." Now everyone knows if you want to know anyone's business or if you need to have any information regarding school activities, Tiffany is definitely the person you go to. To me, she's really annoying, so I keep her as far away from me as possible. *Thank God we're not in the same homeroom class*, is all I'm thinking. Sliding my desk further away from hers, I totally tone her out as we prep for the period to begin.

I'm constantly looking at the clock just above the chalk board. I can hardly concentrate on what my teacher is saying. It really doesn't matter at this point because I already pass this class with flying colors. "Don't forget to collect all your items before leaving my class," the teacher announced. She didn't have to tell me twice because I was already packed and ready to go. You would've thought that I had the bell in my hand how I responding so quickly when it rang.

Speeding down the staircase to get back to my homeroom class, I saw Jacqueline's best friend, Tenaska, entering the class door, so I slowed down midway before stepping into the classroom because I didn't want to seem anxious or excited. Taking deep breaths to slow the pace of my heart rate, I begin to gently tap my face with my hand towel. I stood in the door way looking around, but for some reason, Jacqueline was nowhere to be found. *I wonder where she is?* Thinking to myself. A poke from behind raised the hairs on my eyebrow as a sweet voice whispers, "Who are you looking for?"

"Ahh, I'm just standing here looking at these crazy people in this class." I murmured.

"So what you had to talk to me about?" she aggressively says.

"Well I just want to apologize about last night."

"It was a total misunderstanding," I further exclaim.

For a second, she appeared to be not impressed by what I just said, but she looked up with this shy grin saying, "Don't worry about it, everything cool."

"So that situation is dead, right?" I said.

"Yeah, that's dead." As she giggle.

"Anyway, I'll chat with you later, that was the bell just rang," she utters.

"Cool," firmly saying. I went off walking to my next class with my head held high just grinning from ear to ear. Today just feel so right, potentially having this situation with Jacqueline on lock and the school year soon coming to an end for the summer.

"Wow! Can I get two chicken dinners please," I scream out to the lunch vendors. I hope Jacqueline likes this part of the meat, but anyway if she doesn't I'll take this home for later.

"Hay, what you saying?" I smoothly said entering the classroom with the two dinners in my hand.

"Nothing, we just was about to go and get something to eat," Tenaska aggressively said.

Stunned by the friend's response, I quickly said, "Excuse me, someone was speaking to you?"

Jacqueline instantly intervenes and says, "Drexel, don't mind her. What you saying?"

"Yeah, like I was saying, I bought you something to eat, it's a chicken dinner."

"I hope you like?" I said in a heavy tone of voice.

She takes me by the hand, pulling me away from where her friends are standing, and tells them she'll catch them up.

"Watch how you holding this hand nah," I whispered. With a wicked grin on my face similar to the one like what the twins usually have when they are up to no good. She couldn't help but blush as she kept saying, "Thank you!" We sat in the class for the rest of the time just chatting about our likes and dislikes. Come to find out, we really had quite a few things in common. After the day was done, I hooked up with Nard to catch the bus home. During the whole ride, we were just talking about the playoffs and how we can't wait for the tournament to begin as it was relating, Nard mention if I knew P.J. got a full scholarship to Arkansas. This is one of the twelfth graders that played for our school team this past year, he's pretty good. I figured if it was anyone that was going to get pick it would be him. Standing in the driveway of my yard, I began to vision myself in P.J's position, having the same opportunity to play college ball like he has, and as I'm throwing the ball into the air, allowing it to roll off my fingertips I can hear the crowd going wild chanting aloud, "Let's go, Drexel, let's go Let's go, Drexel, let's go!"

CHAPTER 6

Days grew one on top of the other as me and Jacqueline's relationship became fonder. We even managed to finish the project before our deadline. I think it was the perfect timing for a perfect topic in which helped propel me to a perfect year on being an honor roll student. Today, I could officially say that this final day of my eleventh grade year, I am proud to hand this letter to my Mom that states me, Mr. Drexel Robertson, has maintain a GPA average of three point and above for the entire school year.

"Can you please shut the hell up and let's play ball?" Kane shouted.

"You're just jealous, dude, because you graduated with a one point average for your whole school career," I exclaimed.

"Don't worry, not everyone can be me!" I continued saying.

"Yeah, you're right, no one can be a loser on and off the court like you," Kane exclaimed.

"Why don't you two just quit it and let's jam?" shouts Jermaine.

This is Kane's cousin who just came back from college, I like to call him "Pimp" because he's always wearing this cowboy hat and he's always speaking like an American. Mocking his American slang, I shout, "Pimp, where the females at?"

He always talks about how many white girls he use to have back in Virginia, but honestly I just get a kick out of listening to his college stories. Here comes Nard and his younger brother, Donnie, we call him "Handles" because he's crazy when it comes to dribbling the ball.

"I gat you, Nard, you on our team," I shouted as he makes his way to the court.

"Dude, these kicks are nice!" I admirably said.

"Yeah, bro, these are the same tennis we were looking at that day," Nard replied.

"Aw yeah, they are really fresh bro!" I exclaimed.

"Well when we go away this summer, I'm going to buy me a few pairs of nice kicks also," I further exclaimed.

"Yeah, bring me back a pair when you go!" Kane screamed from the benches.

"Definitely, I'll bring you back something!" I replied.

"A children's book to help you with your reading skills," adding softly.

We played about four games before I decided to make my way home, T didn't come out this evening, but I'll check him a little later on tonight. *I wonder what Jacky saying,* pondering to myself.

"Drexel, I want you to paint the front of the house for me tomorrow," Mom shouts from her bedroom.

Mumbling under my breath, I calmly said, "Yes, Mom."

I wanted to try arranged something with Jacqueline tomorrow, thinking to myself.
"You have something to say, boy?" Mom sternly says.
"No, No, No, Mom," I stuttered saying.
I can't afford to mess this nice period up. I want to stay on Mom's calm side, she really been responding well to me since I brought home that letter from school. I guess she really was impressed.
"Aw, Drexel, one girl called here for you," Mom shouts.
Leaping over Shana playing in the hallway, I pulled up on Mom saying, "Who was it?"
Answering with this disgruntle look on her face, Mom replies, "She said Janet or something, one funny name."
"You mean, Jacqueline?" I anxiously asked.
We both stood in the kitchen giggling as she said, "Boy, you know I can't pronounce these names."
Creeping off with the cordless phone in my hand, I closed the room door and locked it behind me. I place my CD player up on the dresser then searched through my collection for a nice tone to set the mood. Jodeci… No, Boyz to Men…No, R. Kelly…Yeah R. Kelly should be nice. Pitching the volume at a nice level, I then decided to dial the number. Okay the phone is ringing, that's a good sign. A soft voice answers, "Hello."
"Good evening, may I speak with Jacqueline, please," I say with a heavy base in my voice.
"Hold for me," the person replied.
I can hear the footsteps making its way throughout the background; suddenly, a slight hello flows through.

Right away, I knew it was Jacqueline, so I said, "How you doing?"

She replies, "I'm doing fine, Drexel." Listening attentively to her voice, I can picture the look on her face, and of course, she grins when I said, "And you damn sure are fine." Sifting deeper into the conversation, R. Kelly's "Bump and Grind" began playing in the background, and surely gained momentum off of that, but the feedback wasn't what I anticipated. It wasn't as if she rejected me or anything, but she just didn't respond like I thought she would. A beep must've came through on her line because she told me to hold for a second, the second turned into ten minutes, so I hung up. Then I waited another fifteen minutes to see if she would call back, but she didn't.

Two straight days has passed since I've been working on the house and not one single call has come through from Jacqueline. I spoke with T earlier today and he believes I should call her. He told me that I don't know what may have happen that evening. Maybe she got some bad news or maybe her phone is temporarily disconnected. Sometimes, I hate to give in to his thoughts because he always has a theory for a situation, but I guess he's right because I really don't know the reason why. As I'm dialing the number, I'm still a bit hesitant, "Well, so much to the part where T said the phone may be disconnected," I whispered to myself. The phone is clearly on because the line is ringing. It rings at least three times before Jacqueline picks up the line. She pauses when she hears my voice, and then tells me to hold on. She clicks back over to the other line and then returns asking if I was home. I told her, "Yeah, why?"

She answers, "I have to call you right back."

I'm like, "Wow are you serious?"

She says, "Please, Dre, I'm going to call you right back."

"Yeah, okay," responding in disbelief.

I didn't bother to wait around this time. I grabbed my ball, placed on my tennis, and ran as fast as I could to the basketball court. I'm playing like a man possess, no one can say a word to me. Nard came over patting me on the back asking me if I'm all right, but I totally ignored him and continued on playing. After we won two straight games, I sat on the bench just staring across the court. Just vaguely I heard Nard shouting to me that the tournament is starting next week. I nodded my head letting him know that I remembered. Soon after he left, I went back on the court and caught another game. I think it really helped because when I got home I felt 100 percent better.

Moving forward, I never tried calling Jacqueline back and she never return the call she said she would have. I didn't understand where I went wrong, but my guess is that she may have met somebody else. Having the time now to focus on basketball, I worked heavily on my post game. Gaining a few needed pounds, I felt more confident going into the tournament. The advantage we have here is that the tournament allows you to pick your own team of players, so I didn't have to worry about being cut because me and Nard basically formed are own team. Looking at the players on paper, it seems to be an "all star" team, but on the court, we were horrible. We lost our first two games to a team I'm certain we could've beaten. Everybody on the team blamed me for not rebounding and blocking enough balls, but like I told Nard, it's really the team effort that has us losing. I'm already grabbing nine to ten rebounds per game and blocking about two balls every time we play. It's just that everyone wants to shoot the ball. He totally agreed and we decided to switch up some things for the next game. For sure the plan worked, not only did we win the next game, we won two games back to back. The feeling was awesome and everyone began to gel with one another on the team, we were on fire up until the last game. Our team totally collapses and reverted right back to that selfish way of playing, it was humiliating and we lost by a large margin.

During the award ceremony, I kept saying to the guys that it was there stupid playing that caused us to be second runner up, but it didn't faze them none. They just accepted their trophies and went off with a smile. It wouldn't be long after that I'd be going off with a smile because we're preparing to go on a cruise tomorrow morning.

Everyone in the house is packing, but Mom says to pack only the vitals because we would do a small shopping in Florida. I can't wait; I'm a bit exhausted of Nassau. I think a change of scenery would be good for us. The whole night I'm just sorting through clothing trying to find only the things I really need. I look at the clock it's already after one o'clock.

Mom knocks on my door and says, "Drexel, make sure to put yours and Shana's luggage to the front door when your finish."

"Yes Mom!' I said with such excitement.

I take my nice tuxedo down, that's for the captain's ball that occurs on the cruise. I have to look sharp because I never know who I'll meet. Okay, it's now quarter to three and I better wrap it up because I have a long day ahead of me tomorrow. Wow! It feels like I only blink my eyes for a sec before the alarm sounded. Mom is already out the shower, and Shana is getting ready to go in. The sun hasn't rise as yet, so I'm confuse on what time it is. We are schedule for a 7:20 a.m. flight, so my guess is that it's about five o'clock in the morning. The only good thing is that I can sleep comfortably on the plane. I did a quick cowboy and carried the luggage to the vehicle. Now here is where the task gets difficult, trying to fit all these bags in the car.

Mom comes outside saying, "Boy, why you just standing there, put the small ones at the back seat." She aggressively comes over and starts placing each bag one on top of the other. I just follow until all the bags were successfully in the vehicle. Shana had to sit on my lap during the ride to the airport. The ride didn't feel that long because there aren't any cars on the road. On our arrival, there were guys waiting with trolleys to take our luggage to the check in desk, luckily, when we got inside, there were only two persons ahead of us, so we were able to maneuver smoothly through the airport. As we sat in the waiting area for departure, the seats are rapidly beginning to fill, looking at everyone's appearance, I could see that they feel the same way I do—sleepy, but yet excited. At exactly 7:20 a.m. the airline called our flight I looked at Mom as she grabs her bag and told Shana, "Let's go." Both of them with a slight grin on their faces. Making our way to the plane, it felt as if each individual was speed walking. Mom was way ahead of the pack, which was good for me because I was able to join the line where she was standing. Everyone just stared as I went directly in front of the line. Entering the door of the plane, the air instantly changed, our seat numbers were between 13A and 13D, I told Shana I will get the one by the window. She didn't mind because she wanted to be next to Mom, so she sat in the middle seat. I'm literally on top of the world, but for a moment, I think of my dad and how this would be a good opportunity to visit him, especially where we were stopping in the Florida area. Landing at Miami Airport, the air is fresh and the sky is beautiful, cars zooming from left to right. Even from up above, I know deep within myself that this is something I can get use too. I'm like a baller right now in the stores; it's like everything I see I want, but Mom pulls me aside and says, "Put some of those items back."

She further exclaims that I may want to purchase items on the cruise so I need to budget my money properly. She made it quite clear that she wasn't giving me more than I already have. Thinking about it, she was right because when we got on the cruise, I totally lost my mind.

Game room, casino, clubs, food, drinks, and most of all, women—it's like a whole world moving on water.

The lights, the elevators, how in the world you have elevators in a ship? And how many levels does the ship have for elevators to be needed? It's extraordinary and remarkable. With this, you get to see just how wonderful the human minds really are. It's possible for persons having problems, to come on this cruise and fall in love all over again, or in my case, fall in love with a person while being on the cruise.

I'm meeting so many interesting people from all walks of life and cultures. I'm even learning how to speak a little bit of Filipino from this Filipina kid that I met during a contest down by the pools. For once I felt free to roam. And Mom wouldn't get upset about where I was or what time I came in.

"I'm going to the club upstairs." I shouted to Mom as I exit the room.

She says, "Okay, we'll be downstairs getting something to eat."

Standing up fresh from head to toe waiting for the elevator door to open, there is this sweet fragrance that hits me by surprise. I lift my head as the door separates and there she stood; forget about Jasmine Mills, this here officially is the most beautiful girl I've ever seen. Her hair jet black; which rest gently on her back and her body perfectly curved in all the right areas. It's like a ray of sunshine that consumes the space in the elevator. Watching her every move as she converse with a guy and another female, I didn't realize they were all going to the club also, so I build the nerve to ask them if they had ever been to this club since boarding the cruise. The guy said he was just there last night, but the two females said, "No, this is our first time going in." I didn't want to appear too aggressive because I still didn't know the relationship between the gorgeous female and the guy. Eventually, the guy ended up on the dance floor with another female, so my instincts told me that they were not dating. I decided to make a move over to where she was standing and ask if she's enjoying herself here on the cruise.

She replied, "Yes, what about you?"

Intrigue by the response, I calmly said, "Yeah, man, this is nice."

I believe it was a good ice breaker because she then ask, "Where are you from?" Instantly I replied, "From the Bahamas, Nassau to be exact."

In return I said, "So what is your name, if you don't mind me asking?"

"Jenny," she utters as she gently places her hair behind her ears.

"Well it's nice to meet you, Jenny, my name is Drexel," I confidently said.

Everything seems to be going so well as I also learned that she was a Latino. Suddenly, the DJ totally took it up a notch, playing the track, "Lets get Married" by Jagged Edge. I was so nervous to ask if she wanted to dance, it's like I absolutely froze up when the song came on, but she totally flipped the script on me and ask, "Drexel, do you want to dance?" Overwhelmed with joy I shouted, "Yes, I mean yeah, sure!"

The night was so magical I didn't want it to come to an end, she felt so perfect in my arms that for the whole time we were dancing, I was just trembling. Apparently, the guy who she was with was her cousin. They eventually came over and interrupted the moment we were having, saying, "Jenny, it's time for us to leave."

With my hands inter lock with hers I quietly said, *Man, ya'll some party poopers.*" Jenny turned to me and said, "Drexel, I had fun tonight, we'll hang out tomorrow." Strange thing is after that night, we never hang out, with all the activities going on and the ship docking at the different ports, it was like the time blew by. Before I knew it, we were packing our bags getting ready to travel back home, but the experience I had will be one I cherish for a lifetime. I believe everyone is disappointed that we have to leave today because I look at Mom and she doesn't seem to be excited about getting on the plane to go back to Nassau. Shana is over in the corner crying her eyes out as if someone has stolen her favorite toy. Immediately, I go over to her side and console her, letting her know that we'll come back next year and do it all over again.

Both Shana and Mom smiled as we boarded the plane. This time, I allowed Shana to sit by the window while I sat to the one by the isles, it didn't bother me at all because just as we were about to take off, I fell right off to sleep. Wow! I slept for the whole flight. I guess my body is catching up on that rest I didn't get during the trip. It's funny how one minute you could be in a place so far away, and the next minute your home sitting at your dining room table unpacking.

The process of unpacking is the most annoying thing to do after coming off a trip. Pushing my luggage aside, I decided to hit the streets to see what I missed out on, first stop T's, but no one is home. Then I crossed over to Kane's and it appears as if no one is here also, but I hear a rattling sound coming from the door as if someone is trying to open it. It's Pimp and looks like he was asleep. His face is wrenched up like he has just opened his eyes for the first time today.

"Pimp, you just getting up ay?" I asked as I anticipate his American accent.

"Yeah, men, I'm just seeing the light," he answers.

Just as I thought and stronger than ever, the American slang is still there. I'm listening and also laughing at the same time, but in some instances, I could understand why he is so traumatized from the experience because it was a lifelong dream for him—to be able to go to college and graduate with his degree. Every word is like Virginia this, Virginia that. I can barely cut into the conversation where he's going on and on about his buddies. Once again, I take a good look around my neighborhood. Demetrio has just graduated from high school and from the looks of things, it doesn't appear that he has any intension of furthering his education. Kane has been working a year now since graduating from C.H. Reeves High School, and college doesn't seem to be on his mind. It's more about hanging out and wheeling in the females. In fact, he has just bought a nice vehicle to accommodate all the women that he's attempting to capture in his net.

My eyes are slightly open to the possibilities, especially after feeling so at home on the trip; mixing and mingling with such a diverse group of people came natural. I'm finally able to slip away from the conversation because Mom is screaming out my name.

"Anyway, Pimp, we ga talk later," saying as I rush off home.

I guess it is back to my normal program with Mom because we haven't been home a day yet and she's rowing. Tommy appears to be frustrated also because he aggressively stomped out the front door as I entered the house. When I think about the relationship at times, I could sometimes understand why he gets upset—it could be hard dealing with a woman like my mother. As I'm adjusting daily, I find it hard to let go the memories from the cruise. It's just a whole different atmosphere, is what I'm explaining to T, but T can't stop talking about his exciting time he's having especially where he doesn't have to prepare for the upcoming school year. He's a high school graduate now, "What's next for Mr. Gardiner?" I asked.

His eyes drifted upward as if he didn't have a sure answer, but he projected his body up and said in a stern voice, "Well I'm starting the Technical School in September."

"Oh yeah, what are you taking up?" I replied.

"Computer repairs," he answered.

"Then hopefully open a repair store when I'm done," he further explained.

"Wow, dude, that sounds awesome!" I said with a proud look on my face. It was almost like the one you give your son when you know you did a good job raising him. He goes on about his relationship with his girlfriend while I'm just standing, staring, and wondering when I'll have a girl to call my girlfriend, but I'm pushing hard not to allow him to see that I'm a slight bit jealous. I know whenever I come to talk he always listens; no matter what the circumstances are.

CHAPTER 7

A few days slowly passed, and I'm reaching an impatient level of not having a companion, I don't get any calls and I don't have any admirers. I don't want to fall in the category of my cousin. He just likes to come over to my house to watch the porn channels all day. That stuff is just straight up freaky and perverted, he'll never get a woman using that method. Anyway, it's time to release some testosterone. The court is jam-pack and I'm not the happiest person right now, and as I analyze my performance from game to game, I discover that when I'm not laughing and clowning around, my game is a whole lot better. I even got a slight compliment from one of the brothers during the game.

"Hay, what you saying sexy?" Duran screams from the court as we're deep in the heart of a game.

I stop to look also and I totally concur; because the female is really sexy. It appeared that Duran knew the young lady because she waived as her and her friend slowly walked by. This evening, I decide to take a different route home—mainly to see if I could spot the female along the way—and yes, just like I predicted, her and the friend comes walking toward me along the sidewalk. With no hesitation I say, "Hello, how you ladies doing?" They both answered, "We're fine."

Riding the momentum I asked, "Do you guys mind if I walked and talk with ya'll for a minute or two?"

The crazy thing is that the ugly one was acting freaky, having an attitude as if I was bothering her. For me, it's strange because in all my cases, I always get a good response from the ugly females. I don't know if this is a good sign or bad, but I'm willing to try my hand. I walked with the young ladies for a good thirty minutes before we got to her house. The plus is that I know where she lives. Feeling positive as we both said our *good-byes* to one another, I realize I didn't get her phone number, but I'm already half way home and I'm not turning around for a second time.

Tomorrow couldn't come quick enough before I was up showering and getting dress to go around the corner to see if the young lady would be outside. Not to make it look like I was intentionally coming pass her house, I decided to go around the other side of the neighborhood to make it look coincidental. My heart is pounding out of my chest. I'm sweating bullets as I walk through the hot scorching sun, good thing I brought my towel with me.

"Okay, okay," I whisper to myself, and just like I anticipated she's outside on the porch with her friend from yesterday. I pulled this plastic bag from my back pocket and slip my towel inside to make it look like I had just came from the store.

"Hay, sexy, what's going on?" I calmly said.

At first she doesn't hear me, but her friend somehow sees me waiving from the road and taps the young lady on the shoulder, pointing in my direction. Bear in mind that the sun is extremely hot, and I'm standing directly underneath it. I want to pull this towel out the bag so bad, but I know she'll pick up that it isn't groceries that I've been carrying. She stops and stares then in the middle of our conversation she says, "Do you want a hand towel for your face?"

Right away I replied, "Yes!"

"What about a glass of water?" she continues saying.

I grin because she must've seen the exhaustion on my face. I licked my lips and said softly, "I would really appreciate that."

We both chuckle as she told me to come inside. I followed her straight to the kitchen, watching her as she attempts to reach for a glass from the top shelf. Her shirt rises slightly, my eyes open wide as my imagination runs wild. *Man, her skin is nice.* I'm thinking to myself. Before she could turn to look at me I said, "Do you want me to get that for you?" She stumbles back and I quickly catch her from falling. Then she says, "Yeah, it'll probably be much easier for you to reach." The water is definitely a thirst quencher because I feel rejuvenated, watching me carefully she says, "Do you want some more?"

My first thought was to say something smart like, *No, but I would love to have something else.* But I simply said, "No thanks that was good enough."

I handed her the glass and started to make my way to the front door, but before I could step outside, good she shouts, "You could sit down inside, ya know."

With a bit of a hesitation I said, "Okay."

Her friend came inside and said, "Girl, I coming right back," as she shuts the door behind her. Nervous is an understatement to how I feel right now, but I'm pinching my knee to ease my mind. She comes over and sits a few inches away from where I'm seated and says, "Is there anything else I could get you?"

Again, a thought runs through my mind, but I simply replied, "No, I'm straight."

"Ya know something? I never got your name," Quickly, I bounce back saying. She looks me dead in the eye and says, "Ya know something? I never got yours neither."

"Wow, I have a stranger in my house," she further exclaims.

We both laughed, then she stretch forth her hands uttering, "Well, hi my name is Lucy."

As we continued giggling, I eased over to shake her hands and replied in a smooth tone of voice, "I'm Drexel and it's really nice to meet you, Lucy."

For some reason our hands locked and I leaned in even more, everything felt right as I stared at her lips. She began to whisper something that I couldn't understand; I think my mind is completely gone now. My lip eventually touches hers then a sudden *bam, bam, bam* rattles the front door. It's her friend knocking on the door, I think it frighten her because she pitches up from the chair instantly, I can see her chest moving heavy as she breathes.

Her friend steps with a slight grin on her face calmly saying, "Well, well, well."

Lucy pulls her hair back replying, "Girl, what's wrong with you?"

I quickly jump up intervening the two and said, "Anyway, I better make my way home."

Lucy then turns to me with a disappointing look on her face and says, "Are you sure?"

"Yeah, man, I have to take this stuff home," answering with an uncertainty in my voice.

She pulls me aside whispering, "Where exactly do you live?"

With a smirk I reply, "Right opposite the church by the park, the house is white trim with black."

"You were coming round there ay?" I continued saying

"Yeah, give me another hour or so," Lucy utters.

After leaving her yard, I quickly ran home and began fixing up the house. Shana is looking at me like I'm a crazy man, but she doesn't bother to ask what I'm doing because she's enjoying the fact that I'm cleaning up both her and my mess. I sat in the front room area looking through the blinds every split second to see if I'd see her coming up the steps, but for every moment the doorbell rang, it was someone other than her that was coming to the shop.

Two hours pass and no Lucy. It felt like one of those moments again. I can't even call to find out if she's still coming, stupid me didn't ask for the phone contact.

Looking through the cracks of the blinds, I could see Mom pulling into the driveway. I didn't even realize how much time went by where I was so focus on Lucy. The only good thing is that the house is clean and the store made some good money today, so it shouldn't be any complaints coming from Mom. Mom walks through as if she's patrolling the scene, and after she was done, she nods her head like to say, "Good job," but nothing comes out of her mouth. Just as she was about to head to her room, she shouts, "Aw, Drexel, there is a young lady outside to you." I'm like, "Man, Mom how long?"

"Boy, don't mess with me this evening." Honestly, I don't want to get on Mom's wrong side, so I quickly went out the door and there she stood, sweet and sexy as ever, Lucy. The first thing that captures my attention is the perfume fragrance that she's wearing. I'm not that familiar with perfumes, but whatever it is it could surely set a man on fire. I can see that she put some serious time and effort in her appearance because she looks spectacular.

"Wow all this for me?" I smoothly said approaching with my arms spread wide for a hug.

Lucy replies, "What you mean?" *As she embraces me with a warm welcome in her arms.* I have to admit she felt really good in my arms. Slowly stepping back a few inches from her body, I continued holding her hands while saying, "You know what I mean, this look you have right now."

"You like it?" saying as she smiles.

"I'll only like it if it's especially for me."

I don't think I've ever seen a young lady blush that much in my life. She looks down and then slightly looks up into my eyes with her head turn just a bit saying, "Yeah, you're right, I did it just for you."

It was like a little person jumping around inside. Finally, I feel like what I'm doing is actually working.

Words are just flowing off the tip of my tongue, before the evening was out we were making arrangements for tomorrow.

"Anyway, see you later." As both our faces showed great anticipation for what is to come for the following day.

All night I'm planning out what I want to do, hoping and praying that Mom doesn't give me a bunch of chores for tomorrow, and suddenly, she comes knocking on my room door saying, "Drexel, I need for you to go and lock the gate for me, please." Quickly, I leaped from my bed responding, "Yes, Mom!"

Mumbling along the way, "If that is all she wants me to do, that isn't a problem."

Cutting my night short, I found myself up earlier than I expected. Continuing to play it smart, I didn't get out my bed because I can still hear Mom right outside my door getting ready to leave. So far so good, she hasn't come banging on my door to tell me to do some type of chores today. I listened carefully, and I hear her keys jiggling, and the front door slams. A few second goes by before I heard the gate opening. The vehicle starts and she makes her way smoothly out of the yard. Perfect, she's finally gone; now the only task is keeping Shana busy. I don't want be too obvious with the situation because it's quite clear that Shana is sharper than I think she is. As the morning sets in, I decided to catch up with Simone in which she's always roaming the streets, so it's very easy to find her. When I did finally saw her, I asked her where DD was, she said exactly what I wanted to hear, "Home, playing with her makeup set." Now if it's anything that I can bribe a four year old child with, it's with candies and ice cream, and what better place it is to have that leverage, seeing whereas we have a shop filled with goodies. I told Simone that if she tells DD to give Shana a call to come over to her house so that they can play with the dolls and the hair products that she can have any treat from the shop for free. Her face literally lit up like it was the Fourth of July.

Exactly twenty minutes later, Shana receives a call and exactly twenty seconds later, she was packing her hair products, letting me know that she is going by DD to play for a while. Plan executed to perfection, this time I'm ahead of my game, I got the phone contact during our sweet conversation yesterday, it's almost twelve o'clock, but I'll give her another fifteen minutes before I call.

"Hello,"

I replied, "Well, hello."

"Yes, to whom do you want to speak too?"

Oops, I thought it was Lucy who answered the phone, but apparently it's her younger sister.

"Oh, my apologies, can I speak to Lucy please?" saying confidently.

"Sorry, she's not here at the moment." As she abruptly hangs up the phone.

My heart begins to race a thousand beats per second and instantly, I become frustrated with the fact that she isn't home. Yesterday we agreed that we'll meet up roughly around twelve. I waited another fifteen minutes before picking up the phone once again. Just as I'm dialing the number, the doorbell rings and I'm like shucks—Shana is back already. Immediately, I'm devising another plan to get her out the house, I shout, "Shana, you done already ay?" No one answers, so I look through the window to see who it was, but I couldn't view the person from the angle they were standing, but that familiar fragrance hits me by surprise.

"What you saying?" are the first words uttered from Lucy's mouth.

I open the door standing in shock as my heart beats even faster.

"Sorry, is this a bad time?" Lucy figures after seeing the look on my face.

"No, no," I exclaims.

"Sorry, I'm just a bit shock, because I was just trying to call you."

"Awe, I probably had left already to come here," Lucy says.

"Well, never mind that. Please come inside," I sternly say.

My god she is hot, she has on these long tights that stop just above her ankles and this nice colored top with her arms out. Damn, her skin is smooth.

In the same motion of checking out her ass, she slaps me on the shoulder and says, "What are you looking at?"

"Okay, okay, you caught me. Honestly, I'm checking you out," I said as biting my lips intentionally.

"Damn, you look really sweet," I continue saying. Flattered by my compliment, she makes this sexy sound as she laughs. Returning the favor I ask her if she wants anything to drink. As I'm looking from the kitchen into the living room area, she looks even sexier sitting on the couch. I quickly dash over and grab the remote for the stereo and place on my R. Kelly CD, good thing I left it inside the player because it was kind of cool being able to just press play.

Walking over with the glass of water in my hand, she starts to get up to receive the glass from me, but I told her, "No you don't have to get up." I sat down right alongside her saying, "Here you go, my lady."

"Well thank you so much," she replies.

As the music plays softly in the background, I can sense the change in the atmosphere, it totally sets the mood that I'm looking for. Eventually, I eased in for a kiss after she took two sips of her water. She must've sense it also because she met me half way as we're smacking on one another's lips, I feel the nervousness coming from her body. I grab her in closer to my body and she totally accepts everything that I'm doing. Suddenly, R. Kelly's "Bump and Grind" comes on as we're passionately kissing and touching, it felt as if it was over hundred degrees in the house. I placed my hands on her hips and cuff both butt cheeks in the palm of my hands, lifting her onto my body, she suddenly wraps her legs around my waist while I carried her to my bedroom.

Pushing the door open, I manage to grab the remote for the air conditioner, all I'm thinking is, *Thank God for the man who invented remotes.* Launching her onto my bed, I begin to strip her clothing bit by bit, with every touch her body trembles. It seemed like she had come prepared because the panties she has on are see-through. Everything on me is standing at attention; she blushes as she loosens her bra. I gently lay her down on the bed and place my hands on the inside of her panties, the kisses become even more intense. I lean over to my small bureau opening the draw to grab the box of condoms. As I'm looking at her face, she's totally in tune with what's going on. A loud outburst comes from her mouth as I push my special tool inside of her. The warmth from her body sucks me in even more, before I realized it we were in gulp in a serious sex scene and it's happening at every possible angle of my bedroom. This must've been my lucky day because for the whole time we were engaged, Shana never came home.

I'm in my room replaying the whole scene from earlier today, totally feeling myself as I prance round the room. Mom comes in unannounced and says, "What's your problem, why are you stomping around in here?" Overjoyed and excited, I simply laughed it off saying, "Can't wait to get back to school!" Just how fast the days were rolling in was just how much me and Lucy were keeping up with are sexual activities. This carried on until a week before school was officially opening. I don't know if it was me or her, but the feeling is fading away as the summer is coming to an end. Crazy thing is I'm not even upset and from the looks of things, it appears as if she isn't upset either. It's like having the best of both worlds, she doesn't mind being cool with me, plus sharing that intimacy.

CHAPTER 8

Taking on a new leaf in my life, I'm coming to the realization that I will be graduating from high school at the end of this upcoming school year, so I take a moment out to get a few things in order. My shopping is done, and now I'm able to write down a few goals for this school term. Just briefly chatting with T, he expressed how he'll be starting the technical school on Monday also. It made me understand that when you plan to do something, you must also execute. This is exactly what he's doing. I didn't bother to tell him about my dealings with Lucy, especially where it isn't relevant at this moment. It's more like a mentorship that I'm seeking. Before leaving, he says something real interesting, he is like, "Bro, whatever you set your mind to, you can do." I don't know if he knew exactly what he was saying at that very moment, but it help boost my confidence going forward.

It's the night before the opening of school; Mom is shouting, "Make sure to iron all the uniforms because I am not waiting on nobody tomorrow morning."

I think this is the first time I can say that the statement made by Mom, I totally agreed with because I can't afford to be late on the first day of school.

Tearing the plastic off each one of my uniform shirts, I'm thrilled about pressing each and every one of them. After I'm done, I lay out my neatly creased pants and place my nice black Clarks out on the box that I purchase them in. For a good twenty minutes, I stood there just staring at the items repeating over and over, "Boy, I'm going to be fresh tomorrow." Turning slightly to the mirror, smoothing down my freshly cut fade chanting, "This is one fine black dude!" Its official, I'm ready for tomorrow. The sound of my alarm awakens me from my sleep, but I'm not bothered by it at all. My nerves have me up and about, even though it is pitch black outside. I'm up so early, I decided to go and wake Mom up from her sleep. I clip on the light in the hallway and said, 'Hay, hay, hay it's time to get up!" As I continued cutting on all the lights, I began clapping my hands shouting, "Shana, get up and go in the shower." Tommy was just looking like, "What the hell kind of coffee I had to drink this morning?"

It was a good thing that I did get everyone up earlier than expected because we just beat the traffic that was developing on the highway. Seriously, government have to do something about these roads, it's difficult trying to get from one end of the island to the next without bumping into some kind of traffic.

Arriving exactly two minutes after eight o'clock, I see that the school yard is jam-pack with students. I have just a slight feeling of nervousness, but as I make my exit from the vehicle, I begin to calm down. I've been attending this school from the seventh grade, so this was like my backyard. All the females are like, "Look at you, Drexel, you have grown a couple of inches." Understanding the effect I was having on these young ladies, I decided to stroll over where I know Jasmine and her crew usually hangs out. And yes, my plan worked out in my favor, they all looked as I flaunt my stuff.

With so many of the nearby public schools converting to just junior high, we had a lot of students transferring over to our school, so it was a lot of new faces to meet along the corridors. Seeking out the twelfth grade block, I noticed my name listed in the top stream of the twelfth-grade class, not that I'm surprise or anything, but mainly shocked of who all dropped and who all moved up. It's amazing how so many things can change during a summer break. Just about every female in my class looks very mature. I guess I wasn't the only one that was sexually active this past summer. The bell finally rings for class to begin, but the desk I'm seated to is a bit small for me to fit comfortably. In attempt to getting my teacher's attention, my buddy next to me shouts, "Boy, you look like Shaq sitting in that desk, bro!" I didn't think he was that funny, but I just gave him a blank expression and said, "Yeah, dude, I'm trying to change this desk right nah." Ms. Gray allowed me to switch seats with this new student in which whom is obviously in no need to have a desk that size. I thought T was the shortest man in the world, but apparently, he is beaten out by this guy whom is shorter than he is.

Thinking back on last school year, I knew I had some unfinished business to care of. One, being Jacqueline, during break time I went out on a quest to see which homeroom class she was in. Touching base with each one of the classrooms, I was unsuccessful. I manage to glimpse her crazy friend walking through the corridor, boldly I approached and tapped her on the shoulder saying, "What's up, Tenaska?" Surprisingly, she knew my name as she placed her hand by her waist line shouting, "Yeah, Drexel, what do you want?" From what I understood, our last encounter wasn't a good one, but that was because she was too fast on her mouth, so I had to put her in her place. I guess that explains the aggressive tone in her voice. As I attempt to ask her where is Jacqueline, she completely ignores me, but with a little persistence, she finally says, "Jacqueline moved to C.R. Walker High School, in fact she doesn't want to talk to you anyway, so I don't know why you bothered to ask." What I realized is that these two have been having a lot of conversations about me, and maybe it was another situation where we misunderstood one another. Attempting to further the conversation, the bell suddenly rings for our next period to begin. I came up close behind her and whispered, "We gonna chat later." She frowns up her face and rolls her eyes then walks off without responding back to me; all I'm thinking is that this is one crazy girl.

For the first day of school, the work load seems to be very heavy. Teachers waste no time on giving us all kind of assignments to do, so far every class we had today we were given homework. So much for looking fresh for the first day of school because it didn't matter to the teachers how we looked, it was all about what we know and what we were capable of doing.

The first two weeks of school, I found myself bogged down with school work that I could hardly slip in a day of basketball, but in the back of my mind, I'm keen on trying out for this year's basketball team. Mentally and physically, I want to be ready for the challenge, so I decided to allow the church bus to drop me off near the court. Secretly, I manage to squeeze in a little practice session. I neatly rest my shirt across the bench and somehow maneuvered round in my church pants and shoes. After strategically coming up with this plan, I made this an every so often thing for whenever I wanted to work on my game knowing that any other day would be difficult. I'm once again prepping for another Monday morning as I'm stricken with a pain along my thigh area while I'm massaging back and forth. I grin to myself because of this crazy thought running through my mind, *It may just be all those days I was having sex with Lucy that have my body cramping up like this*. I couldn't believe that for the whole time I was spending with Lucy, I didn't play ball. I guess that's how it is when you have a woman messing around with your head, you can't function properly. With the little focus I have left in me, I manage to muster up being selected for an interview for the Deputy Head Boy position—this is a message I received first thing this morning after arriving a few minutes late. I asked Ms. Gomez, my hospitality management teacher, roughly what time they'll be interviewing me.

She replied, "Not sure of the exact time, but it'll probably be during the morning."

Okay, calm down, Dre, you could do this. It's just a few simple questions they are going to ask you, I murmured to myself as I tried to converse with some of my classmates to take my mind off it. Second period during Language class one of the administrators came to the room letting my teacher know that I must report to the office at break time. The only good feeling about this situation is that I wasn't being call to the office for anything bad. Once again I started repeating the words, *Okay, calm down, Dre, you can do this, it's just a few simple questions they want to ask you.* Periodically, I kept repeating this in my head until the bell finally rang for the break time. Entering the office felt so refreshing, the air is so cold I wish I could remain in here for the remainder of the day.

"Well, good morning, Mr. Drexel Robertson," the principal said.

"Good morning, Mrs. Ingraham." Shaking her hand firmly.

As I'm being escorted to the board room, I realized that it wasn't only Mrs. Ingraham doing the interview—it was her, the vice principal, and about six other members from the PTA board—seated on each sides of the room, they began drilling me with ridiculous questions. One after the other, but the one question that stood out for me was when they ask, "What would I tell people about CC Sweeting High School? Now here it is, I'm torn between being dishonest or telling the truth. Honestly, I preferred them giving me multiple choice questions where you just circle the answer A, B, or C.

After juggling all these crazy thoughts of how I can answer, I just took a deep breath and said, "CC Sweeting High School is an institution that needs to penalize students more severely because we have lots of fights here on the campus."

"Well, thank you, Mr. Robertson, for your time, you may head back to your class now," Mrs. Ingraham replied.

"Yes, madam, and thank you too for the opportunity," I uttered softly.

Trying my hardest not to dwell on the interview, I suddenly found myself asking Nards during our bus ride home those same questions, and from my perspective, I feel like I did awesome compared to the way he answered them. I didn't bother telling Mom what occurred today at school—her and Tommy are in a heated argument right now.

Apparently, there is some mix up with the draw in the shop and some money is missing. It seems as if anytime Tommy is managing the store, either the draw comes up short or the draw is over the limit compared to what was sold during that day. But it isn't any of my business, I just grab Shana's hand and tell her to go to her room and do her homework. It's very rare that you find students at the basketball court during the beginning of the school year. I guess where the uniforms are new nobody wants to be dirty looking or smelling stink, but we're already a month into the year and the guys are getting into the groove of bringing their basketballs. Boy, I would love to bring my ball, but that'll be the day hell freezes over. Mom would probably slap the taste from my mouth if she knows I was thinking this right now, even worst if she knew if I was at the court at this very moment.

"In your face, boy!" screaming as I ran across the court after hitting a three pointer, and what better time to do it while everyone is watching. For the first time, I was not the person being laughed at, it was Reno. All across the court, everyone is screaming, "Boy, you let Drexel kill you!" Even though it wasn't a real game, I still felt good because Reno is supposed to be the best player in our school right now. He was on last year's team, and now he's considered a veteran coming into the new school year.

Sweaty and heated is how I'm feeling at this present moment, so I asked my teacher if I could be excused to go to the restroom. Quickly dashing over, I heard a chuckling sound coming from the changing room area of the restroom. Not paying much attention to the sound, I continued dabbing my face with the water, and while pulling the lever for the roll of paper to come out, I heard the sound once again. First, my mind told me to ignore it and hurry back to class, but for some reason, I couldn't resist. Surprise of what I saw that was making this funny sound, there it was three tenth-graders whom were skipping class. Annoyed and disturbed, I began to lecture them about the importance of school and how they shouldn't be sitting here procrastinating. By the time I was done, I was escorting them back to their classes. Of course, I briefly stopped back to my class to let my teacher know what was going on. Being so highly impressed, she allowed me to go with a passing card just in case one of the administrators decided to stop me on the way.

Honestly, I'm not surprise of how I handled the situation, but I must admit that I am shock of how the three boys reacted. Before entering their class they all said, "Thank you." That to me was amazing, and as I journeyed back to my class, I had the three *H* listed across my face; *head held high* with my chest plunged forward. *Taking the risk on doing something positive is better than thinking about the results or reaction because the result or reaction may just surprise you.*

CHAPTER 9

More and more every day, I believe in this way of thinking and as we approach tryouts for the new basketball season, I'm working day in and day out on my game. The level of my school work has gone into another gear based on my end-of-term results. The only thing that was disappointing so far for this school year is that I didn't obtain the position for the deputy head boy roll. I told T jokingly that I was selected to be interviewed for the head boy position; so if he asks again about it I'll tell him it was a tough line up and they elected GPA over charisma.

PE is today, so I manage to slip my basketball into my gym bag without Mom noticing. "Let's go, let's go," shouts Mom. I shove the bag up underneath my armpits quickly brushing pass Mom, throwing the bag into the back trunk of the car. Shana stares at me as if she knows exactly what I'm doing, and knowing her, I can't miss and think that she didn't pick up, so I politely nudged her and told her to be quiet. Giving her the eye—like you better not or I'll kick your—you know what! But instead, she does the total opposite. She shouts, "Mommy! Drexel has—"

And right when she is about to say it Mom says, "Hush, girl, I'm trying to listen to the news."

It's perfect timing because everyone knows that whenever Mom is listening to the news you better not disturb her. I grinned the whole way to school, because between the road rage and the music, Shana never got a chance to say what was on her mind. It's very rare that you find an individual that sincerely cares about your future and the self-development of your being. Ms. Gomez is truly the definition of this statement. I can't believe how she takes time out to help even though she has a busy schedule. Every time we sit and talk she always tells me to be the best I can be, giving vital information about colleges and on future planning. Today is just another of the many days that we've sat and chatted.

"Anyway, Mr. Robertson, that was the bell," Ms. Gomez said.

"Yes, madam, thank you again, Ms. Gomez," I replied with a great deal of satisfaction.

"Put away your text books, we're having a pop quiz today," Mrs. Bridgewater says. She's a new teacher and just about every time we come to her class, we have a pop quiz. Everyone says, "Wherever the hell she came from, she needs to go back." I could hear the whole class bickering as we put our books back into our bags. Usually, I don't mind, but today really isn't the day. We're handed the quiz sheets and she says, "You may begin." I look down onto the sheet and then smile.

It's right up my alley—it's a multiple choice questions. I'm so confident with the answers I finish in less than ten minutes. In fact, I had enough time to look over it twice before she shouted, "Put your pens down and turn your papers face down on the desk."

I looked around as some of the students still weren't finish, short man next to me whispered, "This must be was a speed pop quiz ay."

I'm like, "Yeah, I guess so." I politely turned the other way and began laughing quietly because I'm thinking how much time you really need to do twenty multiple choice questions. As the time draws near for the period to end, I feel this big rush of excitement running through my body.

The next period will be PE, and after that school will be out for the day. What an awesome set up because basketball practice is after school, but before I can dive in fully to that fact, Mrs. Bridgewater gives us a heap of homework to do for tonight and politely says, "Have a nice day class and I'll see you tomorrow Lord's willing."

I don't think its one male in our twelfth grade sector that doesn't like this time of year during PE class because everyone believes that they can ball. As we run certain drills, you can see clearly that the guys are showing off their skills as Coach Barry looks on. This is where he starts to do his analysis of each and every individual, so right after we were done with the drills, he split us up in groups of five, placing certain guys with others, I guess to see how the chemistry may be. I watch how he matched us up and when I got my chance, I took full advantage of it. I knew I was doing something right because after we won the scrimmage game, he came over and said, "Good job, Robertson, you coming out to practice this evening, right?" Playing it cool, I calmly said, "Yes, sir, most definitely!"

Since then every time I came out to practice, I kept repeating the same methods that excited him from that one PE session and it was quite apparent that it worked because on the day that Coach Penial Barry picked the team, I was standing on the right side of the court along with Randy Smith, Elliott Bain, Kendall Jennings, and Baron Taylor. We were definitely a force to reckon with, by mid-season, we had one of the best records in the conference. Amazingly, I was selected to play on the Bahamian High School All-Star Team; it couldn't be going any better than I anticipated. With my character being like a magnet toward everything, I'm able to sustain a position as the President of the Junior Achievers Club.

During a brief chat with Ms. Gomez, I told her that the administration staff will surely regret the choice they made of not choosing me to being Head Boy of this school. She could only laugh as she said, "Drexel, you are too much. But keep that attitude up, you're doing great!" she further exclaimed.

Following up on Ms. Gomez advice, I began researching different colleges for the best basketball programs, even though I had a great season, I still didn't get any scouts attention. Maybe where I just made the team this final year it hindered my development of being that awesome player I know I can be.

As I close my eyes for the night, I am constantly haunted by the horrors of being a failure, so I'm awakened by the disturbance of my dream. It has me soaking wet from the sweat or perhaps that was because of the AC not being on. I stood up and walked gently to the kitchen for a glass of water, and onto the bathroom I go to drain the wizard, by the time I got back to my room, the air condition was already cold. I said a short prayer and dosed right off to sleep.

Sounds of a frying pan sizzling, suddenly grasp the attention of my ears, then slowly it tickles the nostrils of my nose with its appealing scent, reminding me that today is *Good Friday,* and luckily Mom has the day off. Hot cross buns are neatly stacked across the dining room table while Mom and Shana are in the kitchen getting the fish going.

"Um, um, this smells good nah!" I shouted as I'm looking around in the kitchen area.

With a loud outburst, Mom says, "Don't touch nothing in this kitchen, you need to go and clean up yourself." I happily oblige and came right back after I was done. Everything just melts in my mouth as I'm eating the fish along with the hot cross buns.

"Thank you, Mom, the meal was great!" I utter as I'm licking the icing from off my fingers.

Suddenly from the background, Shana screams, "What about me?

"My apologies, thank you too, Shana, for such a wonderful meal," I quickly respond saying.

Shortly after, Mom says that she's going by Aunt Mable for a few minutes to see what they're up to. I told her okay, and ask if she could tell Carlos to give me a call. I wanted to know if him and Uncle Pete started going out on the court as yet. Mom gives me a look as her and Shana makes their way out the door, I guess it was me mentioning the court that slightly ticked her off. Feeling bored, I decided to walk over to Demetrio's house just to kill some time, not surprise that Pimp answers the door. He always gives the impression that this is his house, and sometimes, I truly forget that Kane and Demetrio live here.

Laughing to myself I asked, "Pimp, when you going to find something to do?"

He sucks his teeth and utters, "Nobody wants to pay me for what I'm qualified to do."

I laugh, this time I did it out loud saying, "Where is black boy?" "Who you mean, you mean Demetrio?"

"Boy, pimp, you are really smart and educated," I replied.

Chilling on the front porch with Demetrio and Pimp, we found ourselves taunting one another as went back and forth on who is the darkest person on our block. During this time, the twins happen to show up on the scene, before they can set foot on the porch, good they were already screaming out my name. We all just sat there talking a bunch of foolishness, mainly of how they use to crash my house whenever Mom left to go to work. Then calmly Ron says, "Ya'll know Alex dead, right?" For a minute, my mind went blank, like, "Who is Alex?" Then Demetrio shouts, "You mean long boy who live in Sunset?"

Mon replies with a settle voice. "Yeah, bro, some dudes shoot him over a gambling game."

Then it all came to me that this was one of the guys who we used to play ball with us out on the court.

The twins were really close with him, especially Mon because they went to S.C. McPherson together. If my memory serves me correctly, I don't think he even graduated from high school. In fact, Mon had already gotten expelled from S.C. McPherson. Truthfully, it made me sick to my stomach as I began to picture his face in my mind, he didn't even get to make it out of this community. Demetrio stands up and holds on the pole with his head hanging down then turns to Ron and says, "Ya'll let's walk out front." The twins quickly jump up saying, "Yeah, let's go."

I politely said, "I will see you guys later then." It's not my style of hanging out with these guys. I never felt comfortable with the twins even though we grew up together; they change a lot since they got kicked out their father's house. I remembered them being very athletic; they were good at every sport. I really thought that they would've gone pro in one of the sport, but observing their demeanors' I believe company became their main down fall. It's like Alex, from my knowledge he wasn't a bad guy, he was a very respectful young brother. Most of all, he had a father figure in his house. It was the people that he surrounded himself with and just like that he was caught at the wrong place at the wrong time.

Wanting so bad to share this information with someone, I quickly jogged over to T's house, but from the looks of things, he isn't home either. Putting two and two together, I understood that maybe he and Kane went out. I noticed he's been hanging with Kane, and this guy they call "D" a lot and just lately, Vano told me that T dropped out of the technical school. Boy, I hope he knows what he's doing because I would hate to see him end up like the rest of the males in our community.

Time ticks even faster as I'm nearing the final stretch of high school. The pressure increases, the jokes that were once funny aren't funny anymore. I think I'm slightly losing my mind, I've written over a hundred letters to coaches in the states, and I have yet to receive answers from any of them. *What is wrong with me? Am I not good enough? Will I ever succeed?*

Knowing one place that I can go for a relief, I decided to walk across the street to the church, just to calm my nerves because lately a lot of evil thoughts have been running through my mind. No one in school knows what is going on with me. Ms Gomez called me in her office the other day and asked me how everything was going. I lied and said everything was awesome.

I'm praying asking for the Lord to forgive me, still with holding my tears from falling down my cheeks, it's hard going forward especially when it seem as if there is no hope. The message from the pastor is piercing because it feels like once again he is speaking directly to me, this time I'm not afraid of going up to the altar for prayers. There is nobody stopping me from going, nobody whispering in my ears, it's just me and God. Then suddenly, I black out. At least that is how it felt. I'm surprisingly in my bedroom and I can't remember anything that happened between the time I went to the altar and me being in my bedroom. Confused and frightened, I slowly make my way into mother's room asking, "Mom, did I walk inside the house on my own?"

She squints her face and says, "Boy, come out my room asking me foolishness." As I'm walking off, I could hear her saying to Tommy, "I swear to you something wrong with that child's head." I caught Shana coming out of the bathroom and I asked, "Shana, you saw me come inside from the church across the street?" She answers, "Yeah, what happen to you? Leave me alone, let me go put on my clothes." As she quickly brushes me aside. It's quite clear that I'm not going to get any answers in here, so I settle with the thought that I had a major anxiety attack, and that I totally couldn't recall anything.

After weeks of doing BGCSE exams, I'm made aware that I received a call from a school in Tennessee. Quickly writing down the number, I made it a point to respond as soon as I arrived home. I told Nards the news during our bus ride home. I don't think I allowed him to say a word where I'm so overwhelmed with joy. After getting off at my stop, I practically jogged straight to the house in my school uniform. The adrenalin has my mind intensely racing that I don't even stop to take off my clothing.

Carefully laying the paper with the phone contact out on the kitchen counter, I began dialing one digit at a time. It's an overseas call, so it's taking a few seconds for the call to go through. Moments after, a middle-age lady answers the phone. I'm really excited as I'm explaining to her who I am. She tells me to slow down because she couldn't understand me clearly. I slowly go through the details again and this time she is able to assist. Transferring me directly to an agent that has my files, I'm made aware that I was offered a basketball scholarship to go back in the twelfth grade. The gentleman said the only thing I would have to do is find a house family.

Trying to understand the actual meaning of a House Family, the gentleman kindly explains and it meant that I would have to find a family that reside nearby the school to live in with during the time that I'm attending the school. Patiently awaiting the arrival of Mom, I'm already writing down a few things I would need. As soon as I hear the vehicle pulling in the driveway, I'm caught standing in the doorway to greet her. Mom steps out the vehicle saying, 'Boy, don't just stand there, come and help me with these groceries." My mind is so focus on the scholarship I didn't even realize she had bags in both of her hands, so I rush over and grabbed the rest of the groceries, which were at the back seat of the car. Entering the house, I have a big smile on my face. She looks up and says, "What is your problem, boy?"

I answered, "Well…I have some good news for you!"

"What's that, I could stop working?" she replied.

"Well not yet, but it's something even better."

Saying with such confidence I uttered, "I was offered a scholarship to attend a Christian school in Tennessee. The only thing is I'll have to go back into the twelfth grade again," I further exclaimed. For the whole time I'm explaining she doesn't say a word then she suddenly responds when I said, "And I'll have to find a house family."

Now I don't know if it was the *house* part that triggers her off or if it was the *family* part that took it through the roof, but she is like, "No, you aren't staying with any strangers. Sorry, I can't help you with that. That's out of the question." Before I can explain anything else, she simply refuses to go any further with the conversation.

Stomping off to my room she shouts, "Boy, watch yourself nah."

I instantly try to get a grip of myself, but the minute I got to my room, I exploded. It felt like the walls had caved in on me and I could've cared less if I was dead or alive. Suicide is what I'm contemplating. I begin to knock my head against the wall like a crazy man until I started bleeding from my forehead. No one even comes in the room to check on me. *I am so pathetic,* is all I'm thinking. I cried so much, that I cried myself right off to sleep.

CHAPTER 10

Opening my eyes to a wet gloomy day, I try to prepare myself mentally for my final exams. I don't have a word to say to anyone, and during the long drive to school, I'm in complete silence. I glimpse Mom looking at me through the mirror, but I guess she knows that I'm highly disappointed, so she does the norm and doesn't say a word. I'm consumed by exams for the whole day that I barely get a chance to dwell on my poor excuse of a life. Only God one knows how I made it through the day. A few of my classmates noticed I wasn't myself because when there was a perfect opportunity for me to crack a joke, I didn't give any response.

Every moment felt longer than normal, and instead of me writing down *Words of Life*, I'm now writing down *Words of Darkness* like my fair well letter. Constantly, I'm repeating to myself, *I'm not going to my graduation, I'm not going to my graduation.* I said it so much that I really started to believe it. Until Aunt Mary called, she gave me a serious tongue lashing after what I told her, it must've really ticked her off how I was acting because I've never witness this side of Aunt Mary. I thought T had a way with words, but Auntie went from insult to encouragement. It's like I had drowned and she had come to my rescue to revive me. The perspective she came with gave me a whole ray of hope, and by the next day, I was back writing letters to coaches all across the United States. Thoughts still hinder my forward progress as I'm in preparation for graduation, but the work load helps me daily to sometimes forget.

It's Wednesday evening, and I just came from T's house, the phone rings the same time as I'm entering the door, Shana answers and shouts, "Drexel, telephone!" I'm boggled by whom it could be, I pick up the phone gently saying, "Hello?"

The voice replies, "Well hello, Drexel, what you saying?"

I'm still not able to put a face to the voice, the person then continues saying, "What happen to you, you don't know how to talk to people ay?"

"I'm sorry, but I don't know who I'm speaking with," I confusingly said.

Suddenly, the person attempts to cover the phone, like they didn't want me to hear what was going on in the background. In between the muffle sound, I could slightly hear another voice speaking in the background; the person comes back and says, "You don't know who this is, Drexel?" But before I could respond, the voice in the background shouts to the person on the phone, "Tenaska, stop playing and give me the phone please."

As soon as the person said, "Hi, Dre, how are you doing?" I knew exactly who it was.

"Wow it's been a long time, but I'm good," I said.

"What about you, how you been?" I continued saying.

"Everything cool, ya know," the soft gentle voice replied. She grins as she says, "You know who this ay?"

"Yeah," I quickly replied.

"Aw yeah, who then?" she says.

I laugh and paused for a few seconds to make her believe I didn't know then I said, "This is my sweet and sexy, Jacqueline."

I can hear her blushing as she says, "Whatever, Dre, you know you forgot about me." Stunned by her response, I told her it's the other way around, but she totally denies it and says calmly, "It's complicated." I took a step back and gave her an opportunity to explain.

Everything that I listened too wasn't something I really wanted to hear, but it surely brought clarity to the situation. "So it was your ex that wanted to get back with you?" I said shortly after she explained.

"Yeah," she replied with a guilty tone in her voice.

So I asked, "What's the situation at this present time?"

"Well, we're still together," she replied.

Disturbed by the answer, I quickly said, "So why the call now?"

"Well, Tenaska told me you asked for me and I sent a message back with her, but it was quite obvious you didn't get it."

"My phone was off and I couldn't contact you."

"But I'm by Tenaska right now," she further explains.

"Aw, I didn't know you and her were still cool," I said.

"Yeah, you know me and Tenaska are cousins, right?"

"No, I didn't know that crazy girl is your cousin."

We both laughed until our hearts were content and then after about three hours, we finally said are *good-*

byes. I was not sure if it was for the night or if it was for the rest of my life, but at least it's one situation that I'm able to receive closure.

If I say that I'm happy to know that I try my best not to take anything for granted, it'll probably be an understatement because I'm sitting here in the classroom listening to each student as they say what they are going to do when they graduate and most of the guys are like, "Find myself a job and buy me a nice car."

For sure I know this is not the route I'll be taking. Everyone did that already in my family, and that seems to lead to a life full of regrets. As the teacher goes around the classroom, I'm called upon to express, "What is it that you plan to do after you graduate from high school, Mr. Robertson?" I go through the motions as if I'm a candidate giving a speech to becoming the next prime minister of the Bahamas. It's tasteful and full of passion, but for my peers it was another joke that I was making. They laugh so much that my teacher had to shout at persons to be quiet, but honestly I was being serious.

Tonight is prom, and I'm somewhat excited. The tuxedo I have is top of the line, but I don't have a female to escort me. I attempted to ask Jacqueline that night, but it was quite clear that she is still committed. I even tried asking Jasmine one last time, but again I was unsuccessful, so I'll have to Mack this one out by myself. The crazy thing is that T told me he'll be coming to prom also. Now I know my boy smooth with the talk, but how in the world does he have a date to my school prom and he doesn't even attend CC Sweeting?

In the process of getting dress, I decided to pay him a little visit, and men, dude is really sharp.

"Where the hell are you going dude?" I said being facetious.

He chuckles and says, "What? Do you like?"

"Yeah, bro, she really looks nice!" I said admiring.

"Thanks, man! Me and my cousin got these tailor made," he proudly replied.

Just when I'm about to ask him how is he getting to the prom, a stretch limo pulls up in the front of the yard, the driver even steps out to open the door for him.

"What the garbage!" I uttered to myself.

He is like, "Yeah, bro, I have to head out for my date!"

"Anyway, bro, how you getting to the prom?" he continue saying.

"Well, Mom is going to take me there," I said unashamed.

"Cool! Well I'll see you there, bro." Patting me on the back as he rushes out the door.

I wasn't surprise how he responded when I told him how I was getting there because he never really looks at things from that perspective.

Having the approach of a *whatever* kind of attitude, I arrive shortly before the crowd started dialing in. I walked alongside a few of my female friends to make it look like I was with them. Suddenly, as we're making our way onto the red carpet, the bystanders that are viewing the scene began shouting and screaming, "Boy, you look good, gone then." Some even ask us to stop and pose. It's hilarious because I wasn't with any of them, but it surely made out for a good photo. As I'm waiting to see the rest of my classmates in their attire, I spot the pearly white stretch limo that was in front of T's house earlier, not sure if it's him because I'm seeing so many flashy vehicle pulling on the scene. Just as the driver steps out of the limo, I recognize the gentleman from earlier and it is T and his date. The people are making way more noise for them than they were for anyone else so far, it's amazing how much pictures he's getting, even Kane, Nado, and Omar are out there to greet him. T didn't tell me he was inviting all of his staff mates. *Boy, he has a full entourage out here supporting him.* I whispered to myself.

I push through the crowd of people to meet him to the stairway and I have to admit his date really looks hot tonight. I'm not a big fan of hers because she's a bit strange, but I'll give it to her just for the evening.

"Look at, shorty!" I shouted.

You could tell he was happy to see a familiar face because he immediately said, "Hay, bro, where you sitting?"

I replied, "I'm not sure how they have us seated inside."

Then his date rudely interrupts saying," Drexel isn't sitting with us?"

I totally ignored her and said, "I really can't sit with you guys, because I have a few females over on the other side waiting for me"

Music echoed from the interior of the building as everyone made their way to the ballroom, I coincidentally bump into Jasmine as I'm entering the door and just as I thought, she comes in with a date that doesn't even attend our school.

This looks like this was the thing for this year's prom, but unfortunately, I wasn't hip to the memo. I eventually end up sitting with the ugly group in the twelfth grade because the females I escorted while I was walking along the side walk had found their dates. The night isn't so bad as I ate till my heart is content. I took a quick look across the room to see how my boy, T, is doing and he appears to be having just as much fun as I am.

A muffle sound comes from the speakers hanging from the wall as if someone is picking up a microphone and suddenly.

"Now for the main event," the speaker announces.

Before the speaker could say another word, the room goes crazy with noise.

"Then resuming after, a dance off," he continued saying.

All I heard was, "Aw, yeah!" from the persons sitting next to me.

I'm like, "Girl, I want to dance with you!" Winking my eyes as I pull on the whiskers from my chin.

First, they announced the prom king, and I totally didn't agree, but the ladies sitting next to me were screaming like a celebrity had just entered the room. I didn't see why and it's not like I'm saying it should've been me, but from my perspective, I believe I looked better. Now on the other hand, I didn't have a problem with them announcing Jasmine Mills being the prom queen. It's not because of an ongoing crush that I have toward her, but truthfully she looks amazing in that dress. She surely hit it on the nail with that one.

I still happen to enjoy my evening with some of my classmates on the dance floor, even though I wasn't awarded anything.

"You ready to hit the dance floor, Drexel?" Tiffany shouts from behind me.

For starters, I didn't mind because I strategically figured I could work my way up the ladder. All I needed was to snatch one and then move on from that point. If it's one thing I know about a dance floor is that you just have to start dancing and then everyone gets in the mood. I discovered this during our JA boat cruise. Let alone the Key Club Parties.

"Go, Drexel! Go, Drexel!" Is all I can hear coming from the background.

Once again, my plan is perfectly executed because midway through the night, I'm receiving lap dances from a few of the Sexiest female in the building. I even manage to shake a leg with the prom queen. I know it's only because we formed a Soul Train line.

I noticed I didn't see T seated at his chair anymore, and apparently, the young lady he is with isn't there either, so with my inquisitive mind I decided to slip away for a quick sec to check out what was going on.

Rambling through the crowd of people became a slight bit annoying, and just when I'm about to give up looking for him, I see the midget with the shiny silver shirt standing over in the lobby section of the hotel.

"Shorty, what's going on, man? I didn't see you on the dance floor," I screamed over the noisy crowd.

"Yeah, bro, it's getting late and I have to get this young lady home at a certain time," he replied.

Even though I couldn't hear him very clear, I could see he's anxious to go. Her peoples probably strange too.

"Dude, it's only eleven o'clock," I shouted.

He hushes me and whispers, "Yeah, I know, bro, but her mother made sure told me to have her home by 12:30 a.m."

"In actuality, she meant 12 a.m., but figured she would give me thirty minutes to get to their house," he added.

I could only laugh because I know she was strange from long time. I just went along with the program for his sake.

"Anyway, cool we'll talk later," I said as I made my way back to the ballroom.

Scrambling back wasn't so difficult, I guess because everyone seems to be heading to the rooms upstairs.

"Wow! These guys are carrying on bad," I uttered to myself.

Attempting to catch a few females on a slunk, I pranced around on the dance floor to snatch up the weakest link, so I eased up on Tiffany seeing whereas she asked me to dance earlier. I whisper in her ears from behind then all of sudden, she turns around with this shocking look on her face, slapping me across the shoulder and says. "Boy, Drexel, don't play with me. I live by the rules of the seven B's. Book Before Boys Because Boys Bring Babies."

CHAPTER 11

The recover from a week ago is finally making a smooth transition and now it's only two days remaining before graduation. I have yet to receive any response from the colleges; nevertheless, I look forward to celebrating on graduation night.

Today was a blast; my school shirt is sign by just about every twelfth grader in the school, mainly females because that's how cool I am. The most significant signature on my shirt belongs to Jasmine Mills, and it reads, "No you were not the coolest, but you surely were the kindest person and I appreciate you for that. Wish you all the best love Jasmine." And it has a nice smiley face alongside her name. Wow, no one knows how much I've faced in the last couple of months especially Mom, but I know she is proud of me, I can tell by the look on her face as she stares at my report card. It has to the bottom of the sheet reading, "Drexel Robertson is an excellent student with a great deal of awesome work ethics, please continue to encourage him in all his future endeavors."

"Your graduation is tomorrow evening, right?" Mom said.

"Yes, Mom, it's at 7:30 p.m., but the teachers want us to be there for 7:00," I replied.

And that was it; she didn't say anything about the report card. I went to bed with the thought that I'll be officially finish with High School tomorrow. It played on my mind so much that I didn't sleep comfortably the whole night; it was like the feeling you get when you're traveling the next morning and suddenly I'm caught watching highlight of the NBA finals between the Indiana Pacers and the Los Angeles Lakers. Today is free day, so I can relax; I decided to give Lucy a call to see what she was up to. We converse for about two hours before saying she had to go because she had to pick up a few items for her mother.

I admit I'm a bit disappointed that I didn't get to see her, but at least she gave me that much time. The doorbell rings and the person screams, "Come to the shop." I hate it when this bell rings, it's very annoying.

"Yeah, what you need?" I said aggressively to the customer.

"Can I get…" this is another part I hate because persons never seem to know what they want. As I'm serving the customer, a burgundy Toyota Corolla pulls up in the front of the yard. I don't pay it any mind, but as the person makes there exit from the vehicle, I realized it was Lucy.

"Well hello, Drexel," she said emphasizing my name at the end.

"Wow, I wasn't expecting this," I humbly replied.

"I know, that is why I did it," saying with this wicked grin on her face.

"You look like you up to something," I hesitantly said.
"I am," she quickly responded.
We both pause for a moment then she looked over my shoulder; it almost seems as if she's looking to see if anybody is around.
She whispers, "Come closer." I step in as she tips toes, wrapping her hands around my neck and then gently pressing her lips against mine. The feeling is amazing, closing my eyes as I collect each one of the shocking waves running through my body.
Slowly separating I said, "What was that for?"
"That was my way of saying congratulations," she replied and then she gave me another smack on the lips saying, "This one is for me personally."
Before I can say anything, she runs off shouting, "I have to go, we'll chat later, enjoy your evening."
Humored by what had just occurred, Shana comes screaming to the front door, "I'm going to tell Mommy you were kissing a girl in the front of the yard." Totally ignoring as she teases, I began preparing for the evening. It's like the first day of school all over again. Hanging up my neatly ironed shirt and pants, with my shoes carefully positioned on the box that I purchased them in. Yes indeed, I am ready for the tonight.
Mom arrives 5:00 on the button. She must've gotten off early today because usually she gets off at five, and I know with the traffic it's impossible to reach home exactly on the hour.
I wondered, *do I sense a small piece of excitement coming from Mom?* She has her hair fix and a shopping bag in her hand.

Time moves swiftly as we all were ready well in advance. The nerve starts to set in once again; the distance from the parking lot to the hotel isn't far, so I can see the crowd of students standing outside the building. Quickly, I joined in as we admired one another's apparel, cracking jokes and wondering who would go home with the most awards.

Mom pulls me to the side just before she goes in to be seated, she begins fixing my collar and everyone says, "Awe, mamma's boy." For some reason it didn't bother me that they were calling me a mamma's boy because I felt proud to know that my mother is here watching me graduate from high school.

At exactly 7:30 p.m., the Vice principal began calling us in to take our seats, the atmosphere is like the runway for the award shows—cameras were flashing from every angle and people waiving their hands trying to get the attention of relatives as we carefully walk in. It is nerve wrecking, but I made it safely to my position without tripping over a classmate foot.

Before getting started, the whole room is told to stand for the singing of the National Anthem. As I'm singing along with my classmates, the nerve in my body becomes more and more relax. By the time we were done singing, I'm completely locked into my element. Speakers shared their views on life after graduation, while others tried to humor us with stale jokes. Then are most informative student, Tiffany, gives her speech. I've never listen to her before, but this particular time was very piercing and heartfelt in which captured every ones attention. To prove this fact, when she said her closing remarks, the building just erupted as she made her way back to her seat. The vice principal comes to the podium in a very solemn mood then says, "Let's hear it once again for our very own Tiffany Newman."

"Now for the part you've been waiting for," he further exclaims.

I looked around and saw everyone pulling out their cameras. I even saw a parent pulling out a pot and a stick to beat with. Soon after, the names of some of our brightest student were being called up for the most prestige's awards. It got so loud in the room that you could hardly hear what the vice principal was saying. The vice principal announced to the audience that he would need them to save their applause until after reading off the awards. It was very difficult because most of the parents couldn't keep their composure. The edge of my seat is taking a serious chafing as I gear up for my name to be called. Then finally, the vice principal says, "This person needs no introduction, he is a young man that stands in a league of his own, earning himself the award of the most helping and reliable student on our campus, his name is none other than." And every one in the twelfth grade along with the vice principal screamed, "Drexel Robertson!" The noise in the room was enough to blow the roof off. I looked at Mom as she stood up to snap a picture of me receiving my awards. It was the most emotions I've ever witness coming from my mom, her eyes lit up like a kid on Christmas Day, she was definitely proud of my accomplishment. This was the one time I didn't mind her not saying a word because the words were obviously written all over her face.

CHAPTER 12

It's a big adjustment being out of school because now, definitely, the pressure is on. I figured if nobody gave a crap while I was in school then certainly it'll be worst with me being out. Daily, I can hear tiny voices whispering, "You're not going to be shit in life." As I constantly seek a response from the letters I've been writing. It's officially six hundred letters that I've written, and not a single mail has been answered.

Every day, the window of opportunity feels like its closing on me, and suicide lingers in the shadows of my being, so my only option is to continue searching for a job because if I plan to do anything pertaining to college, I am going to need to have my finances in place. I never knew how difficult it was looking for a job. The last few weeks have been hectic, so far all the business establishments that I've visited are saying, "Sorry, but we are not hiring at the moment."

If I haven't heard that a million times, then I haven't heard it at all.

"Now you understand what I was saying to you, Dre," Pimp shouts.

I know I shouldn't be indulging in this conversation, but Pimp seems to be connecting totally with what I'm experiencing and instead I respond by saying, "Yeah, I see why you still home."

He flicks a mosquito from off his shoulder uttering, "And, boy, that's me with a degree."

Once again, a thought runs through my mind like, *Why in the world I having this kind of conversation with this, dude, because when I really think about it neither of us are helping one another.*

Suddenly, I start picturing myself looking like him. With a hairy face and a cowboy hat tilted to the side of my head chilling on the patio with nothing to do, so instantly, I say to him I have to go, even though he was still carrying on a full conversation. I needed some positive energy in my system, but the fast pace of life seem to have consumed T because he's hardly home. Vano and I just decided to sit and talk for the rest of the afternoon, which turned out to be a bit healthier for me.

Rolling into another weekend, I mark the calendar as the weeks quickly go by. Amazingly, a month has pass since graduation and still I have not gotten use to the fact. As I'm digging through the kitchen cupboard, I slightly hear a voice screaming out my name, at least I think it was my name I heard, so I tell Shana to turn the volume down on the television for a second to see if I actually was hearing correctly, and yes, surprisingly, it was T shouting from the back of the yard. Vano apparently told him I was there yesterday. Wow! He's really looking different now these days.

"Hay, shorty, what you saying?" I said.

He sucks his teeth like he usually does and says, "Man, right here, tired as hell."

Seeing him up closer, it appears like he even had a slight hang over, so I said, "Boy, you reach in late last night ay?"

"Yeah, bro, we were to a party out Sky Line Drive," he replied.

Now to my knowledge, Sky Line Drive is what you'll call a *high class* neighborhood, so me being the naïve person in this situation, began thinking that there were a whole heap of white girls to the party, but as he explains, my thoughts were actually right on point.

For a brief moment, I wondered why he never asks me if I wanted to go, but I didn't bother to ask.

He then says, "One dude even threatened me at the party."

First thing, I'm thinking is this sound like another *Alex* situation because I don't look at T as being a bad boy, but maybe because he's hanging out with the wrong crowd he possibly can find himself caught in the wrong situation at the wrong time.

He brushes it off and says, "Everything straight with that situation though."

"That was sorted out before we left," he continued saying.

He didn't bother to go into any details and I didn't want to be an accomplice to anything that may have occurred, so I totally breeze by that part of the conversation and continued on to something else.

With no vacation trips plan and nothing to look forward to, I decided to join the tournament once again this summer to somehow utilize my time, but the feeling for the tournament isn't the same as last year. I guess because of the purpose that I was doing it for and now it seems like it's all in vain.

Monday swiftly goes by, Tuesday is a rainy day, and here comes Wednesday with its boring self. I'm caught in my room playing sad tunes on the key board, suddenly, Shana comes barging through my door to tell me the phone is for me. I'm so out of it I didn't even realize that it was ringing. I picked up the line with a depress sound in my voice saying, "Hello."

"Yes hello, Mr. Robertson?" the person replied.

Slowly I uttered, "Yes, this is he."

"My name is Raquel Gomez and I'm calling from the Nassau Marriott Hotel," The person firmly stated.

"Okay?" I hesitantly said. Wondering, *Why in the world somebody is calling me from the hotel.*

She in turn says, "We would like to meet with you for an interview. When would be a good time for you to come in?" she further exclaims.

Now I know back in the days, I use to play prank calls on Demetrio and Vano and I figured that they were just as bored as I was so I politely said, "Well, Raquel, I don't know who put you up to this, but now really isn't a good time."

"Well, Mr. Robertson, your information was passed down to me from my aunt, Ms. Gomez from CC Sweeting," she calmly replies.

"She asked if I could assist in helping you get a job at the hotel seeing whereas I work in the Human Resource Department," she further exclaimed.

I'm like, "Wow, Ms. Gomez is your Auntie? Man, that's my favorite teacher,"

She laughs and then says, "Yes, sir, so when can you come in?"

"Right now," I answered.

"Well I have an eleven o'clock appointment, so how does one o'clock sound?" she said.

"That sounds perfect, so one o'clock it is," I replied.

I'm so excited I arrived at the hotel an hour before my appointment. In essence, I really didn't have anything to do, so I didn't mind waiting. Realizing that this was a breakthrough moment for me, I confidently took the bull by the horns and landed myself a job as a busboy to the hotel. Right away, I began setting some goals for myself and that was to either save to go to college, or save to get a nice vehicle. Constantly, I carried the same attitude I had when I was in high school, and every time my supervisor asks me to do something, I did it to perfection. I did so well in the first four months of being on the job, that I was promoted to the assistant manager position in the Guest Services Department.

Life is feeling good right now as I continue to meet people from all over the world and with the hotel being at its busiest season, the females are pouring in from door to door. I told my supervisor I don't mind working every day of the week if needed, most of the individuals I work with are much older anyway, but on the same note, I'm learning a lot from the old school. It's this one older lady in particular that always has a lot to say because she's been working here for years, so I guess she feels like she owns the place. Sometimes she really cracks me up on how young she tries to make herself look, but honestly, she really needs to try and work on her feet—those toes are horrible. All I'm thinking is that I hope she wear socks whenever she's around her companion.

Before swiping my card to knock off for the day, I briefly stopped by the cafeteria to get a bite to eat, I work so hard today that I forgot to take my lunch break. The crazy thing is that this is becoming a normal thing for me because every evening, the ladies in the kitchen always put out my favorite cake.

"Hay, Mama D," I shouted standing brisk leaning over the counter.

"Hay, boo, what you saying? We have your cake right down to the end there," Mama D replied.

"Yeah, I see it, I really appreciate that," I said grabbing a cup of water and a big plate of food.

She grins because she knows exactly how I go when it comes to my food.

After I'm done, I dread going back upstairs to swipe out. My eyes are weary and my stomach is full to capacity.

"Oh, Tracy, can you please swipe me out when you get upstairs?" I murmured.

I happened to bump into her while she was exiting the restroom and she's going right to same department.

"Yeah, sure that isn't a problem," she replied.

"Okay, thank you!" I uttered.

"You coming out tomorrow night, right?" she shouts as she's going up the staircase.

"Yeah, man, same place, same time," I shouted.

The walk to the parking lot seems like a mile away, and I'm so eager to get there that I have the keys ready in my hand to just unlock and start, so I can zoom off to my destination.

Oozing into a brand new day, I decide to manage my time a little bit different especially seeing whereas we're hanging out later after work. I think everywhere in Nassau, people usually slack off on their jobs on a Friday afternoon, not saying that I am one to do so, but I can't help but sing along with my co-workers.

"Work them right and keep them coming."

"Coming, coming, coming," were the words we all were chanting. We harmonize the words to that song so much that when we got to the club Tracy went over to the DJ and told him to spin that one time for us.

My co-workers and I are having such a blast that a couple of the guys wanted to head over to the Zoo afterwards to keep the fire burning, so I suggested to a few of the tourist that were staying at the hotel that the Zoo is another good spot to hang out.

"Hay, Drexel, I riding with you, bro," Larry shouts as we're walking over to the parking lot.

"No problem, but bear in mind my buggy takes a while to warm up," I replied.

As I unlock the doors for the crew to get in, I cross my fingers hoping the vehicle kicks right over.

I turn the key, and yes, with one crank she starts. I tap my hands on the dashboard saying quietly, "Way to go, baby."

I took my CD face out of the case and cranked on the music. The ladies are definitely feeling it because they're bobbing their heads.

"Boy, Drexel, you have all the ladies going crazy for you!" Larry shouts from the backseat of the car.

As I turn slightly to answer him, everything suddenly goes dim. I blacked out for few seconds then I flashed back in hearing a loud *bam* coming from the rear of the vehicle.

The car is sliding out of control across the pavement, and I can't get a grip of the wheel.

"What in the world!" Is what I'm screaming inside. It's like everything is happening so fast, but at the same time going in slow motion.

Everyone in the backseat is screaming to the top of their lungs. Finally, we hit a tree about twenty feet into the bush that brought us to an abrupt stop. I looked around asking if everyone is all right, nobody answers. Maybe they're in shock.

I manage to force the driver door open and from what I'm able to see, it appears as if everyone is okay.

Persons came rushing over to see if we had any injuries while others were either calling the ambulance or calling the police. I think everyone is a bit shaken up by the impact. Luckily, it isn't any serious injuries to the passengers in the other vehicle, but from the police report, they were apparently driving under the influence, so as far as charges are concerned, the driver of the vehicle will be collecting all. The only thing that had to be discussed was the damages done to my vehicle and they agreed that their insurance will take care of it.

I'm still in amazement of how I walked away without a scratch on my back because from the impact, I thought we were all dead. I stared in the mirror for a good twenty minutes after calming down in the shower and truly I was speared. I started to wonder where I was going wrong because I suddenly saw myself spiraling out of control and from my reflection. It was like I was becoming like every other dude in my community.

Right outside the bathroom door all I can hear is Mom shouting, "This stupid black boy!" And Tommy is saying, "That's why you need to let him stay right here to attend the local college."

"Boy, you are not going to drive me crazy," Mom screams as she stomps throughout the house.

"If you want to kill yourself then that's on you," she continued to say.

This has to be the longest night of my life because I can hardly sleep. I keep repeating the accident over and over in my head.

Wow! I guess I did fell off to sleep at some point because the light is shining bright outside, but I still feel a bit restless. I decide to make myself a hot cup of tea and I ended up on a slow walk over by Vano. Surprisingly, T answers the door, so we all sat and talked. The words that were being exchange between the three of us gave us an overall view of areas that we were falling short in and we agreed that we really need to get it together.

"So, listen here, where do you see yourself in another five years?" T utters.

Honestly, he caught me off guard with that question, but I buckled in firmly then replied, "Graduating with my first degree from college."

"Well, don't you dare procrastinate," Vano screams from down the hallway.

It was something we could laugh at now, but last night it wasn't so funny.

As I'm heading back home, I decided to grab a pen and a pad to start writing once again because when I think about it, I've been procrastinating for the last the six months.

Vigorously, I try to overcome the hurdles in my life as Mom constantly reminds me why she thinks I'll end up like my dad.

"Who she thinks is going to end up like him?" I screamed.

"Who she thinks is going to end up like him?" I scream once again as we trot through the quiet neighborhood.

"Hush, bro, it's really late," T whispered.

"Lord, I cry out to you this night and forever more. I lay my trust in your hands seeking daily to find myself through you, only you understand me Lord, only you brought me to this point in which I stand. Father as you continue to breathe life in my body I shall not be unsuccessful or a jail bird like my earthly father, instead, I will be what you have call me to be. Amen! And amen!

"This became the prayer I prayed every night," I said as T preps the video camera to record.

"Come on, bro!"

"Bring the camera up closer, so the viewer can be able to see me clear because that last one was really blurry," I continued saying.

I can see he's really not in the mood because I had to beg him to come out tonight.

"Bro, how much more of these clippings are you going to send?" He murmurs.

"As many as it takes!" I said slapping my hands passionately against the backboard.

"You're talking about video clippings, you should see how much letters I have already written for the past year and half, bro," I continued saying.

"You know how much letters I already friggin' wrote, bro?" I continued shouting.

"Calm down, big brother," T screamed over the top of my voice.

Suddenly, one of the police officers came outside shouting, "Ya'll keep it down out here for I put both of you in the cell tonight."

We both shouting in one vocal tone, "Yes, sir, no problem."

I sat down in the center of the court saying softly, "I wrote over thirteen hundred letters to different coaches asking for the opportunity to just try out for their basketball team, bro,"

"Just try outs," I gently repeated.

"T" didn't bother to say a word since that point. After that night, he just humbly came out every single time, even though he may have been annoyed. A couple of times, we played a little one on one, but I deleted those clippings of him beating me because I had to make this look as good as possible.

Before leaving the house this morning, I ask Mom if she needs anything to deposit to the bank, because I was going to Scotia today. She replies, "No, but you could bring me back something!"

I laughed as I headed off to work.

I've been in a great mood these past couple of weeks, so nothing much is bothering me.

I finally got news that I was accepted to this college in Missouri, but the finances weren't fully there at the time, but I'm going to sit down with my financial advisor today and see where I'm situated.

"This year going fast, bro," Larry shouts.

"Yeah, you right. It's already summer again," I replied with a restless tone in my voice.

"Well, child, I can't wait to go on vacation next month," Tracy announced.

During my banking hour, I sat down and talk with my banker and from the looks of things, the progress is awesome. I smiled to myself as me and Larry was leaving.

"I manage to get some information these last few weeks, so it's starting to look like the right timing, dude," I said to Larry during our drive back to work.

"Well, do what you feel like your heart is telling you to do, bro," Larry replied.

"You don't want to get stuck here just working at this hotel for the rest of your life," Larry continued saying.

That's all I needed to hear. The remainder of the day, I contemplated what I should do. And after sorting through my mind and talking to the Lord, I spoke to my supervisor and he granted me a week off to handle my business. I went directly home after work and I briefly had a discussion with Mom telling her that I'm going to take the risk and visit Missouri Valley College in Kansas City. She thought I was joking, but I didn't care, I just was telling her out of respect and not really for her opinion.

I bought my travel ticket after making contact with one of the assistant coaches at the school and they agreed that they'll pick me up from the airport when I arrive.

I have never been so excited in my life I'm finally getting the opportunity I've always been waiting for. Mom agrees to drop me to the airport in the morning, but she plugs in that she doesn't have any money to give me. I didn't mind because I had my own money.

I'm up early this morning to catch my flight. And as we're making our way to the airport the car is completely quiet, Mom doesn't say a word not until we reach the entrance of the airport.

"Make sure call me when you reach," she said as I'm exiting the vehicle.

"Most definitely," I replied.

Everything is going smooth it was just a slight delay on one of my connecting flights, but I arrived safely. To top it off, the coach is standing by the baggage claim area with a sign in his hand with my name printed on it, along with two beautiful white females.

"What the garbage," I whispered.

I am highly impressed and instantly I feel right at home. There are a few other guys that are trying out also, but I don't mind because I'm going to give it my best shot.

For a full week, I consistently showed off my skills at what you would call "Open Gym," and by the end of that week, Coach Glyndon was impressed. He said he's seen great potential in me, so he's going to offer me a scholarship pending I got accepted into the college.

I told him I took an entrance exam, but he said I would also need my SAT exam documents stating a score of 950 and above.

It's like, *I'm right there*, thinking to myself.

He probably sense what I was feeling because he calmly says, "Don't worry about it, son, we'll get you straight."

After we were done with the drills, all the guys decided to just stay in for the night. I didn't mind because my body is really tired, so I went right off to sleep.

In relations to being accepted to a college, Coach Glyndon was able to retrieve some information while trying to help, and he saw that I was accepted to another college, right in the state of Missouri. So he promised that he'll work from that end in making sure I get in that particular school to play basketball.

My world is definitely spinning now, the second I landed in Nassau; I made an appointment to the American Embassy to get my student visa. I told Mom all about the trip and what was going on, but for some reason, she still didn't believe me. I even mentioned it to Kane and Demetrio those how excited I was, but they just laughed their heads off.

I kept all of this in my mind as I stood on the line downtown for eleven straight hours waiting to get my student visa saying over and over to myself, *I am going off to college. I am going off to college.*

"Boy, Drexel, you really black nah," Shana screams after I entered the door from a long day at the embassy.

"Just like your pa," I whispered.

Mom was standing there, so I had to be careful. After I got settle in, I then laid everything out on the table for Mom proving to her that I was leaving for college along with my ticket which was booked for August 9, 2002.

I've never in my life experience a season like this, but the blessings that are reigning down on me have me on cloud nine. It's nothing no one can say to me, to make me feel worthless. I have six thousand dollars in my wallet, a backpack on my shoulder, and a one way ticket into Missouri.

Just before Mom pulls off to leave the airport, she gives me a hug and says, "Make sure call me when you reach." I glance back as I'm walking away, and to my surprise, I see that same look she gave me on the night of my graduation.

CPSIA information can be obtained
at www.ICGtesting.com
Printed in the USA
LVOW04s0233131216
517027LV00011B/596/P

9 781628 542134